T0195814

What Christians Should Know and Ought to Do

Dr. Olubunmi Aluko

WESTBOW
PRESS®
A DIVISION OF THOMAS NELSON
& ZONDERVAN

WestBow Press books may be ordered through booksellers or by contacting:

WestBow Press
A Division of Thomas Nelson & Zondervan
1663 Liberty Drive
Bloomington, IN 47403
www.westbowpress.com
1 (866) 928-1240

Scripture taken from the King James Bible.

Scripture taken from the New King James Version®. Copyright © 1982 by Thomas Nelson. Used by permission. All rights reserved.

ISBN: 978-1-9736-7312-5 (sc)
ISBN: 978-1-9736-7313-2 (hc)
ISBN: 978-1-9736-7311-8 (e)

Library of Congress Control Number: 2019913752

Print information available on the last page.

WestBow Press rev. date: 09/19/2019

This book is an in-depth spiritual disbursement of how-to self-delivery. Deliverance is a spiritual exercise every child of God (every born-again Christian) must perform constantly or regularly.

The writer of this book is aware of the fact that many Christians, including those who have been in the church for decades, still work and toil under very difficult bondage and servility; they aren't enjoying their God-given freedom and liberty as found in John 8:36. "Therefore if the Son makes you free, you shall be free indeed." Satan's desire is to keep God's people in perpetuity of bondage and yoke. This book is a wake-up call for every Christian to submit himself or herself to self-deliverance in accordance to the epistle of Paul to the Romans 12:2, calling on all Christians to renew their minds daily and to be transformed. Dr. Olubunmi Aluko is very passionate about seeing the children of God living in the freedom of being delivered from the pain and hurt of Satanic yokes and bondage. Deliverance is quintessential to robust Christian living and successful service as prayerfully outlined and flawlessly articulated in this book.

—Pastor Alexander Oni

Acknowledgments

I would like to say thank you to the following:

My family, who have been supporting me all these years while I teach and pray with different people God has brought into my life.

My dear friends, who have allowed me to use the stories of our spiritual journey together in this book.

My pastor, William Farina, who has consistently taught the undiluted word of God, which has contributed to my knowledge and boldness to teach others.

Opening Statement

This book is strictly for Christians. If you aren't sure you're a Christian—that is, you have no definite memory of when you gave your life to Jesus Christ or when you rededicated your life to Jesus Christ, you may need to stop reading and proceed to the last chapter. Follow the step-by-step instructions, which will establish your relationship with Jesus Christ. If you are a Christian, it's also expedient to rededicate your life at this point before proceeding further.

Introduction

It was in my father's living room in a small village in one of the African countries. I remember a family meeting, where I was the cause of pain and anxiety for everybody. The whole room was stunned by what they had just heard me say. It was less than thirty days to my wedding, and here was I, telling them I had broken off my engagement and was calling off the wedding. Every single person had a question for me, and I answered each one convincingly in my own eyes, but no one seemed to understand me.

A big argument ensued, and my mother was more concerned about what she would tell all her friends. She had already ordered a uniform of traditional wear for the whole family and her friends. She collected money from family and friends. She and some of my sisters traveled to another village to have the traditional costume made for the occasion. She asked me what she should tell all these people, while another person asked me what they would do with all the non-fresh foods that had been bought for the two-day ceremony (that is, the traditional wedding and then the church wedding and reception). These questions went on and on, and I grew angry, feeling like no one was concerned about me; they were all worried about how this event would affect them. My father, however, stepped in and asked us to calm down and pray.

I want to say that at this point in my life, I had been a Christian for about ten years; my mom, dad, and at least four of my sisters and some nieces and nephews had given their lives to Christ and were born-again Christians. My anger dissipated when I heard my youngest sister praying and weeping, saying, "Lord, this is a reproach. This is a disgrace, Lord," and my mom joined in the weeping. I started thinking and praying along with them, and I remember asking God to take away the disgrace—not for my sake but for the sake of these people, who loved me so much and wanted good things for me.

I left to go back to my station, where I worked as a physical therapist in a teaching hospital. On the way, I was ruminating on all that had happened and started asking God some questions, especially why. What was happening that had caused my family (even my younger sisters) distress? Why was the issue so big to them?

The Lord reminded me of another scene in the same living room nine years earlier. This time there had been only four of us, including my parents and brother. They had asked me about the young man I was dating. He was a Christian and a year-four medical student in the medical school I was attending. My parents had fallen in love with him because he visited my dad in the hospital and in rehab after my dad had a motor vehicle accident and had sustained a fracture of his femur. He also came with his friends just to spend time with him. I told them I had broken my relationship with him, and my reason was that he wasn't growing in the faith. That reason wasn't satisfactory to my brother, and we argued to the point that my brother said he gave up on me.

This memory made me sober, and I realized there was a problem here. In the nine years between these two occurrences, I had dated and considered a few other men with three marriage proposals. My youngest sister I alluded to as weeping and praying was the one who had introduced me to one of the suitors I turned down. No wonder she felt something was amiss, and this behavior was getting worse and was now becoming a reproach. I started pondering these past relationships, and I still believed I have a good and cogent reason for each relationship that didn't lead to expectations. However, the pain and supposedly shame I would bring to my family when they must break the news to the extended family and friends convinced me to seek the face of God.

That was the beginning of a deeper walk with God and the understanding of some spiritual knowledge that birthed this book. It is based on personal experiences and how the Lord has used these experiences to open the eyes of many people and how they have been helped repeatedly.

As you proceed with reading this book, I want you to note any area of your life that isn't satisfactory or pleasing to you. Focus on some issues that have been long outstanding and have become accepted in defeat, including the issues you have battled in the past and have given up on. Many times we mistakenly assume it's the will of God for us to lack or suffer after we have prayed and believed to no avail. We also rationalize and think God is saying no to our request. My expectation is that the knowledge you will derive from this book and the experiences of others who put it into practice and obtained their victories will provide a road map or solution to your long-standing issues. I strongly believe that nothing happens in the physical realm alone; many things happen in the spiritual realm before they manifest in the physical realm. If we have physical and spiritual bodies, then we ought to address every situation physically and spiritually. When we take care of the physical body, let's take care of the spiritual body as well.

I was a young Christian woman, who was doing well academically and professionally. I had no financial or health problem, but I couldn't maintain a relationship with the opposite sex for too long, even when all my friends were married and having children. I was a chief bridesmaid five times, but I started losing touch with my married friends because I felt pressured by their concerns and questions. Many people around me believed I was too proud or ambitious. My mother thought I wasn't nice to the young men. I gravitated toward other unmarried young ladies and became friends with them, and we started a prayer group. They started getting married, and I thought this time I would get it right because we had been praying, and the girls were getting their victories. Sure enough, I became engaged again, and this time everything was going as expected until a few weeks before the wedding. An incident happened, and it scared me to the extent that I realized I couldn't go on with the wedding plans. I struggled with telling people for a few days, but every day was drawing closer to the wedding, so I had to act quickly.

I left home to attend a prayer retreat on the supposed wedding day. A friend invited me to accompany her to this retreat; the same day was the anniversary of her husband's death in a motor vehicle accident, and they had been married for only ninety days. During this retreat, we received promises from the Lord that were mainly exciting for my friend. We came home, and that week she got engaged to a friend she has been seeing.

I was flabbergasted by how powerful and effective the prayer retreat turned out to be. That led me to change my prayers to asking for an insight into the problem. I specifically asked for the secret of this problem. When two of us prayed, one heard from God, and the answer happened instantly. But why did the other (me) not hear anything? If God was an all-knowing God, then he ought to know my problem and reveal it. He proved himself true to his word, and each time I prayed, the words *leviathan spirit* would come to mind. This made me realize the problem wasn't just physical; I was dealing with a spirit here, which had become a spiritual problem that must be addressed spiritually.

Self-Deliverance

What Is Deliverance, and Why Is It a Must-Know and Must-Do for All Christians?

The word *deliverance* may evoke a picture of people doing deliverance for someone who is acting crazy, or it may remind readers of a room that becomes chaotic or a picture of priest doing exorcism. My experience and the deliverance that will be discussed in this book are far from what you may be conjuring in your mind right now. The difference is that the one who needs deliverance is the same person who will be doing the deliverance. It is called "self-deliverance" for that reason. In many cases, deliverance is always necessitated by a yearning for freedom or a longing for the betterment of a person's lot in life. The desire and willingness of the party make the experience readily achievable with smooth sailing most of the time.

"But He turned and said to Peter, 'Get behind Me, Satan! You are an offense to Me, for you are not mindful of the things of God, but the things of men'" (Matthew 16:23). This is Satan trying to attack Jesus and weaken his resolution to do the will of God and fulfill the purpose of his coming to the world. Jesus rebuked Satan and cast him away from himself. I recognize this was Satan, though Satan was speaking through Peter. Jesus did self-deliverance when he asked Satan to get away from him.

> Then Jesus was led up by the Spirit into the wilderness to be tempted by the devil. And when He had fasted forty days and forty nights, afterward He was hungry. Now when the tempter came to Him, he said, "If You are the Son of God, command that these stones become bread."

> But He answered and said, "It is written, 'Man shall not live by bread alone, but by every word that proceeds from the mouth of God.'"

> Then the devil took Him up into the holy city, set Him on the pinnacle of the temple, and said to Him, "If You are the Son of God, throw Yourself down. For it is written: 'He shall give His angels charge over you,' and, 'In their hands they shall bear you up, Lest you dash your foot against a stone.'" Jesus said to him, "It is written again, 'You shall not tempt the Lord your God.'" Again, the devil took Him up on an exceedingly high mountain, and showed Him all the kingdoms of the world and their glory. And he said to Him, "All these things I will give You if You will fall down and worship me." Then Jesus said to him, "Away with you, Satan! For it is written, 'You shall

worship the Lord your God, and Him only you shall serve."' Then the devil left Him, and behold, angels came and ministered to Him. (Matthew 4:1–11)

Jesus was able to resist Satan each time by using the word of God. Satan, however, persisted until Jesus cast him away the third time, as indicated in verse 9. I bet Satan would have kept going on and on if Jesus hadn't taken the initiative to ask him to leave. Jesus took personal responsibility to free himself of any influence of Satan on his life and ministry. We all can do likewise; we can ask Satan to leave just like Jesus did. That is self-deliverance. We have the same authority Jesus has, and we can use this authority to free ourselves from all activities of the devil in any form, both internal and external. "Most assuredly, I say to you, he who believes in Me, the works that I do he will do also; and greater works than these he will do, because I go to My Father" (John 14:12),

We live in a changed world where Christianity is no longer revered. One of the reasons is the absence of evidence of victory in the life of many Christians. The majority of non-Christians see nothing worthy to desire or aspire to in the life of the professing Christians around them. In fact, they see themselves as even better and enjoying life more than the so-called Christians. In fact, someone asked me before (and I quote), "What have you to show for your age and this faith in Jesus?" I had no answer, because he was referring to a specific area of my life that was already giving me concerns. It is high time we began to live triumphant lives and get rid of all the hindrances to the victorious lifestyle we have available in Christ Jesus. This we can do only when we come to the realization that we have a problem and understand what type of problem it is.

What Is Deliverance?

This is the act of setting someone free from something that restricts or burdens; it is the state of being liberated or rescued. It is also translated as the act of legal transfer of right or title. We can therefore see ourselves as people needing to be rescued from any burden or restriction as well as legally taking back what is rightfully ours in Christ.

"But He was wounded for our transgressions, he was bruised for our iniquities; the chastisement for our peace was upon Him, and by His stripes we are healed" (Isaiah 53:5).

We know the death of Jesus Christ has provided everything we need to live a joyous, victorious, peaceful, and triumphant life. The pertinent questions to ask therefore are, Why is this fact not evident in our lives as children of God? Why are we struggling or lacking all or some of these benefits?

The reason is that we believe Jesus did the complete work and that we have nothing to do. However, we have a part to play in our deliverance. I would like to compare it to the work of salvation, which Jesus also completed on the cross, but we still must go to Jesus and confess with our mouths that he died on the cross for our sins and accept him as our Lord and Savior to be saved. Many people know about Jesus and what he accomplished, but if they don't confess him, they remain unsaved. We must individually appropriate to ourselves every work Jesus did for us.

Salvation isn't automatic, healing isn't automatic, and deliverance isn't automatic. We all have our parts to play in possessing our possessions.

What Do Christians Need Deliverance From?

A few of those things that restrict or hold us captive, as listed below, will be addressed in this book:

1. Curses
2. Oppression by an evil spirit
3. Sickness
4. Possession by an evil spirit
5. Barrenness
6. Habitual sins or addictive sins

What Is a Curse?

A curse is a prayer for harm to come upon one. The Bible is full of blessings, but there are also many curses in the Bible. A popular passage that enumerates these is Deuteronomy 28. To understand these curses, we must understand the blessings. There are conditions that open the door for these blessings to come upon us. In the same manner, there are conditions that will prevent the blessing from reaching us and then open the door for the curses to prevail in our lives. It's impossible to have the blessings and curses at the same time. The lack of the blessings signifies there's a curse on one's life.

Now it shall come to pass, if you diligently obey the voice of the Lord your God, to observe carefully all His commandments which I command you today, that the Lord your God will set you high above all nations of the earth. And all these blessings shall come upon you and overtake you, because you obey the voice of the Lord your God:

Blessed shall you be in the city, and blessed shall you be in the country.

Blessed shall be the fruit of your body, the produce of your ground and the increase of your herds, the increase of your cattle and the offspring of your flocks.

Blessed shall be your basket and your kneading bowl.

Blessed shall you be when you come in, and blessed shall you be when you go out.

The Lord will cause your enemies who rise against you to be defeated before your face; they shall come out against you one way and flee before you seven ways.

The Lord will command the blessing on you in your storehouses and in all to which you set your hand, and He will bless you in the land which the Lord your God is giving you.

The Lord will establish you as a holy people to Himself, just as He has sworn to you, if you keep the commandments of the Lord your God and walk in His ways. Then all peoples of the earth shall see that you are called by the name of the Lord, and they shall be afraid of you. And the Lord will grant you plenty of goods, in the fruit of your body, in the increase of your livestock, and in the produce of your ground, in the land of which the Lord swore to your fathers to give you. The Lord will open to you His good treasure, the heavens, to give the rain to your land in its season, and to bless all the work of your hand. You shall lend to many nations, but you shall not borrow. And the Lord will make you the head and not the tail; you shall be above only, and not be beneath, if you heed the commandments of the Lord your God, which I command you today, and are careful to observe them. So you shall not turn aside from any of the words which I command you this day, to the right or the left, to go after other gods to serve them. (Deuteronomy 28:1–14)

However, if one lacks any significant number or all these blessings in his or her life, that person will be miserable and won't be able to fulfill any purpose in his or her lifetime. In fact, if all these blessing are absent in one's life, it is definite that there is a curse in operation in that person's life.

I'm not going to list the curses in this chapter, but they are enumerated in Deuteronomy 28:15– 68. The curses mentioned there are almost directly opposite the blessings in Deuteronomy 28:1–13; typical examples are the blessing in verse 7 and the curse in verse 25.

> The Lord will cause your enemies who rise against you to be defeated before your face; they shall come out against you one way and flee before you seven ways. (v. 7)

> The Lord will cause you to be defeated before your enemies; you shall go out one way against them and flee seven ways before them; and you shall become troublesome to all the kingdoms of the earth. (v. 25)

It is therefore right to say that the conditions that bring blessings into one's life are the same that will keep the curses away from one's life. This passage repeatedly explains the conditions for blessings and curses. "Now it shall come to pass, if you diligently obey the voice of the Lord your God, to observe carefully all His commandments which I command you today, that the Lord your God will set you high above all nations of the earth." (v. 1)

Obey the Lord and keep his commandments. This idea is mentioned again and again in verses 2, 9, 13, and 14. On the other hand, disobedience, indifference to the word of God, or going after other gods will close the doors of his blessings and consequently usher in curses. It's easier to prevent a curse than to break one. If a curse is already in existence, there is a need for deliverance. There are a few types of curses.

Individual Curse

This is a curse that is consequential to an individual's sin of disobedience and evil practices. This was first reported in the book of Genesis when Adam and Eve disobeyed God in the Garden of Eden by eating from the forbidden tree of life. The consequential curse was the following:

> Then to Adam He said, "Because you have heeded the voice of your wife, and have eaten from the tree of which I commanded you, saying, 'You shall not eat of it': "Cursed is the ground for your sake; In toil you shall eat of it All the days of your life. Both thorns and thistles it shall bring forth for you, And you shall eat the herb of the field. In the sweat of your face you shall eat bread Till you return to the ground, For out of it you were taken; For dust you are, And to dust you shall return." (Genesis 3:17–19)

It is paramount to note that the word *commandment* is mentioned in verse 17. These curses come because of direct disobedience to God's instructions.

The first example I can recount that is associated with an

individual curse is the story of a young lady I will refer to as Sharon. She was visiting this country, and a friend of mine called me from the Caribbean, asking me to host her and help make sure she has a good time. Once I consulted with my family, and we agreed, I called my friend to let her know my decision. She then requested that I should pray and counsel her because she was a fine Christian, but nothing seemed to be working out for her. I raised a prayer request about her at the prayer meeting I had with six other ladies. My prayer was that my family would be a blessing to her and that I would be able to give her good counsel. One of these ladies had a dream, even before Sharon arrived, and she saw her holding hands with a young man. She said it was like they had a covenant with each other.

When Sharon arrived, I started praying with her and learned she was thirty-three years old; she was going to school in the Caribbean but had abandoned it before completion to go to school in the UK. Before she could complete the program in the UK, the government shut down the school, accusing it of visa-fraudulent activities. She moved in with her cousin in another town in the UK. The cousin died unexpectedly, and she had to move in with the cousin's friend. Sharon couldn't transfer to another school in the UK because the visa request had been denied. She moved back to the Caribbean without accomplishing any significant progress and was staying with family members. Nothing seemed to be working for her, and she came to the United States with the intention of staying illegally. When I narrated the dream to her and said I felt it was the cause of her problem, she confessed that she had been in a relationship with a guy on and off for the past ten years. We realized that due to living in sin, she was responsible for her problem. Though she is a Christian, she needs to stop living in sin; she needs to discontinue the relationship and break the curse that this action has brought on her.

She did self-deliverance, discontinued the relationship, and followed all the guidance God had given her including going back to her country and not becoming an illegal resident. Sharon was obedient; she went back to her country. Within two months she was able to move out from the family member's home and rent her own apartment. She returned to school and didn't have to start from the beginning but was given some credits for some of the classes she'd taken years ago. Exactly fourteen months after she got back home, she was married to one of her college mates in the UK. They are from the same country; they reconnected, and he was able to come home to marry her. Now married, she can go back to the UK legally and complete the educational program online.

Let's look at another individual curse that is worthy of taking note of in the book of Samuel. Eli was the judge in Israel, but he was getting old, and his children were running the show in his place. But their lifestyles and behavior were displeasing to God, and God responded accordingly.

> Then a man of God came to Eli and said to him,
> "Thus says the Lord: 'Did I not clearly reveal
> Myself to the house of your father when they were
> in Egypt in Pharaoh's house? Did I not choose
> him out of all the tribes of Israel to be My priest,

to offer upon My altar, to burn incense, and to wear an ephod before Me? And did I not give to the house of your father all the offerings of the children of Israel made by fire? Why do you kick at My sacrifice and My offering which I have commanded in My dwelling place, and honor your sons more than Me, to make yourselves fat with the best of all the offerings of Israel My people?' Therefore the Lord God of Israel says: 'I said indeed that your house and the house of your father would walk before Me forever.' But now the Lord says: 'Far be it from Me; for those who honor Me I will honor, and those who despise Me shall be lightly esteemed. Behold, the days are coming that I will cut off your arm and the arm of your father's house, so that there will not be an old man in your house. And you will see an enemy in My dwelling place, despite all the good which God does for Israel. And there shall not be an old man in your house forever. But any of your men whom I do not cut off from My altar shall consume your eyes and grieve your heart. And all the descendants of your house shall die in the flower of their age.'" (1 Samuel 2:27–33)

The word *command* or *commandment* appears in verse 29 again. It's obvious the young men lived in direct disobedience to the word and precepts of God for their role as priest. The judgment of God in response to their disobedience wasn't a single act that affected the ones who committed the actual sin. The immediate consequence was the death of four members of this family in one day. This went beyond the people involved and the people closely associated with them at that time in history. Verse 32 reported that the judgment was forever for this family. Forever is unlimited in space; it is an unending judgment on this family. This judgment is passed to the people coming after them. That brings us to the next type of curse.

Generational Curse

This is an inherited curse. The person suffering here isn't the one who committed the sin of disobedience but is partaking in the punishment passed down from older relatives or generation as stated in the word of God.

The first and fundamental generational curse is the Adamic curse that was passed to every human being. The sin of Adam was imputed to every person on earth, male and female. No one is exempt from the consequences of this sin, which is death. In addition to this fundamental curse, many people also inherited other curses from their parents. The Adamic curse requires a remedy; so do other generational curses require a remedy.

> Therefore, just as through one man sin entered the world, and death through sin, and thus death spread to all men, because all sinned—(For

until the law sin was in the world, but sin is not imputed when there is no law) Nevertheless death reigned from Adam to Moses, even over those who had not sinned according to the likeness of the transgression of Adam, who is a type of Him who was to come. (Romans 5:12–14)

You shall not bow down to them nor serve them. For I, the Lord your God, am a jealous God, visiting the iniquity of the fathers upon the children to the third and fourth generations of those who hate Me. (Deuteronomy 5:9)

The story of Eli and his sons alludes to this principle. Verses 32–33 say, "And there shall not be an old man in the house forever / and all the increase of thine house shall die in the flower of their age." Let us visualize a family where there is no one growing old; they die when they are blossoming. A family like that would experience sorrow repeatedly. They would also be accustomed to fear and anxiety because they would know whatever joy they had wouldn't last. This may sound just like a story in the Bible, but it's happening in this present day. A friend of mine called me from another country, very shaken and distraught. She was soliciting prayer for her husband. The husband's older brother had just died at age fifty-nine; he was one of the pillars of the family. The reason her sorrow was so much was because she reminded me that her father-in-law had died when he was fifty-nine years old, which I was aware of. She, however, told me two uncles had also died at that age.

Obviously, something was very wrong with this family. Her husband would hit the mark of fifty-nine in about two years. I can imagine the fear gripping this family. She was afraid not only for her husband but also for the brothers-in-law and her own sons. I can also identify a senior college mate who was diagnosed with cancer at age forty-two. While I was full of faith and hope, he was very resigned to death right from the onset; he kept telling me I didn't understand. I didn't understand his lack of faith and unwillingness to fight for his life. I later learned at his funeral that the older brother had earlier died at the same age, and it seemed like this was the pattern in this family.

The last example I will share happened in my life. I became aware of a pattern of occurrences that was breaking my heart. I noticed that people I loved and had helped in one way or the other turned against me and attacked me behind my back; some dealt with me treacherously, and the experience was very painful. Around this time, a friend called me from Europe and narrated a dream she had about me. In the dream, I had skin cancer, which had metastasized to brain cancer, and I died.

I was troubled because I had a growth on my lower neck I was already worried about. I started praying, and I had a dream of my own, that the same people brought me a dish of burned casserole, and I was fighting them and rejecting it. I knew these people had already done some evil deeds to kill me with cancer. I went to God in prayer, asking why and what I had done wrong. Each time I prayed, my great-grandfather's nickname dropped in my spirit. Though I didn't know him personally, his nickname was strangely distinct, and it registered indelibly in one's mind. I prayed further and got the impression that what was happening to me was because of some atrocities he had committed. I knew I had to deal with the sins of my great-grandfather to stop the attacks, and the Holy Spirit led me.

I shared this matter with one of my sisters just so she would be aware of it. Some years later she called to let me know my only living grand-uncle had turned one hundred years old. At the celebration he shared with the whole family that his dad, my great-grandfather, had been a very evil man, a warrior who'd attacked and killed innocent people and committed many atrocities that aren't appropriate for this book. My sister called me to confirm that the Holy Spirit had been right when he attributed the attack to my great-grandfather. I realized that those people had attacked me because of my great-grandfather's actions, and there was the strong likelihood of a curse on this guy, a curse many of us have suffered for, and some are still suffering for it. He attacked and killed innocent people, for which I innocently suffered a retribution. My great-uncle's reason for gathering the family together was that he was the last of his generation and would die soon, so he seized the opportunity to tell the whole family, including extended members, to accept Jesus as their Savior, especially the non-Christians, because they would suffer the consequence of this man's evil actions.

This grand-uncle was one of the first renowned Christians in my village in Nigeria. He remains an evangelist even in his old age; he has been living a successful Christian life, worthy of emulation, and has enjoyed many desirable blessings. He is still alive at the time of writing this book; he is over 100 years old, while his wife lived to be 98 years. He enjoys good health and a sound mind, so much so that he could be telling people to accept Jesus as their Savior at his old age. He had a knowledge of generational curses and shared with people the secret of dealing with them.

Externally Invoked Curse

This type of curse is self-explanatory. It is a curse someone placed on another person or the whole family. It is usually invoked by someone who felt wronged and had an evil spiritual power. The invoker called a curse down for vengeance because of a perceived wrong done. This type of curse can also become a generational curse. This isn't usually caused by a Christian because it is uncharacteristic of Jesus, our Lord, whose message is forgiveness. "And forgive us our debts, As we forgive our debtors. For if you forgive men their trespasses, your heavenly Father will also forgive you. But if you do not forgive men their trespasses, neither will your Father forgive your trespasses" (Matthew 6:12, 14–15).

If there is a curse invoked on you, it isn't from a Christian, because the Lord doesn't honor such prayer requests; nor does he want to do such things. He made it clear that we need to forgive; this is nonnegotiable. Christians, please don't invoke curses on anyone; you won't help the cause Jesus wants us to hand the battle over to him and to just forgive. He is the one who will fight our battle for us. It is when we forgive in obedience to our Lord and do good to our enemies that we allow our Father to fight our battles for us. Forgiving your enemy won't stop God from judging the case in your favor. Your enemy won't go free or unpunished, so rest assured that the Lord will fight your battle for you at the right time. He attested to this fact in his word.

"Beloved, do not avenge yourselves, but rather give place to wrath; for it is written, 'Vengeance is Mine, I will repay,' says the Lord. Therefore 'If your enemy is hungry, feed him; If he is thirsty, give him a drink; For in so doing you will heap coals of fire on his head.' Do not be overcome by evil, but overcome evil with good" (Romans 12:19–21).

Every curse can be broken, but either it is invoked on you, or you brought it on yourself by your actions. The forgiving grace and power of Christ is abundant, and you can be delivered from all curses and consequential afflictions.

Oppression by the Evil Spirit

Oppression means a sense of being weighed down in body or mind. Oppression from the devil will manifest in different manners. The following list isn't exhaustive, but I will address a few ways the devil oppresses people. There are other types of oppression outside the context of this discussion, such as political or economic oppression. This book is limited to the ways the devil oppresses people, as mentioned in the book of Acts. "How God anointed Jesus of Nazareth with the Holy Spirit and with power, who went about doing good and healing all who were oppressed by the devil, for God was with Him" (Acts 10:38).

1. Physical oppression

2. Emotional oppression
3. Mental oppression
4. Spiritual oppression

Physical oppression means to be oppressed in the physical body, such that the body isn't functioning at maximum potential. This can manifest as body sickness, but the root of the problem is oppression from the devil. A good example was reported in the book of Matthew. "And when they had come to the multitude, a man came to Him, kneeling down to Him and saying, 'Lord, have mercy on my son, for he is an epileptic and suffers severely; for he often falls into the fire and often into the water. So I brought him to Your disciples, but they could not cure him.' Then Jesus answered and said, 'O faithless and perverse generation, how long shall I be with you? How long shall I bear with you? Bring him here to Me.' And Jesus rebuked the demon, and it came out of him; and the child was cured from that very hour" (Matthew 17:14–18).

This boy's symptoms are comparable to the manifestation of someone suffering from epilepsy or a seizure disorder in terms of a medical diagnosis. In fact, the New International Version translation of the Bible reports them as seizures. "When they came to the crowd, a man approached Jesus and knelt before him. 'Lord, have mercy on my son,' he said. 'He has seizures and is suffering greatly. He often falls into the fire or into the water'" (Matthew 17:14–15).

However, Jesus didn't treat this case as the other cases of people in need of physical healing. Instead he addressed the devil by rebuking him. The devil left, and the boy was cured. Certainly some medical or physical sicknesses and infirmities may not be because of a specific disease but because a manifestation of the devil oppressing the individual. This is related to a physical attack by evil people. Satanists, witches, and wizards can attack a person by sending a demon to oppress in different areas and can even send the spirit of death to kill.

My brother's sister in-law was in her early thirties when she became sick. I will like to refer to her as Francisca. She lived not too far from me back in Nigeria when I worked at the hospital. The husband called me to the house because Francisca was walking into the wall as if she couldn't see the wall, and he knew something was wrong. Nigeria has no medical emergency service, so he wanted my opinion on what could be wrong and help to transport her to the hospital. The diagnosis was a stroke with paralysis on the right side, and we believed it was a medical problem according to the diagnosis. However, when we started praying, some things started happening. This change alerted us to address the spiritual aspect. The husband had a dream that a family member very close to the wife saw her recuperating well after she was discharged from the hospital. The family member was surprised to see her recovery, called her by name, and said, "So you didn't die, I planned to kill you completely."

We became very sure that this wasn't an ordinary medical stroke; it was a spiritual attack from the devil, and it manifested as a physical sickness. The agent the devil used was that family member. We dealt with this attack as the Holy Spirit led us, especially praying that we would send the attack back to sender. A day or so later, I got a phone call from the family member in the evening, asking me to call the pastor to come and pray for her. We got there, and she was lying on the couch, saying she couldn't move her right side. She described the same symptoms Francisca had. I asked whether we should take her to the hospital, but she refused, saying all she needed was prayer.

This incident further confirmed that the attack was from her. We kept praying as we were led, and we also followed the strategy laid out by the Holy Spirit. After this event, I went back to the hospital and joined Francisca in agreement for self-deliverance but didn't tell her about the involvement of her family member. While she was still in the hospital, her faith rose, and she told me she would start eating the following day. She was going to tell the doctors to take out the feeding tube; I said, "Amen" because it sounded like an answer to prayer to me. I returned the following day to visit, as I was doing daily; I saw that she had water and pudding on the table by her hospital bed. Francisca reported that she had passed the swallowing test and ate real, solid food that afternoon. She recovered completely after some weeks in rehab, and there were no lingering symptoms. In fact, she came back from a follow-up from the neurologist one day, and she called me to testify that the doctor had reported that she didn't look at all like the person documented in her chart.

I remember a young lady in my old church back in my country; I will call her Pauline. She was having miscarriages or still births in late-term pregnancies, usually around seven or eight months. She would be okay until she woke one day and couldn't feel the baby's movement. By the time she got to the doctor, the baby was dead. This event happened three times, and she was getting depressed. Many people were praying for her, and some from her church knew witches were attacking her. They couldn't tell her, but they were discussing the issue among themselves.

The last still birth was widely broadcasted, and people felt sorry for her. I called her to greet her and decided to speak to her mother, who was taking care of her. The mother shared that her daughter had been suffering and having a lot of breast pain because there was no baby for her to feed. She painted a picture of someone who was beaten, defeated, and almost destroyed. My spirit was very burdened; I wept to God, asking why a child of God, the King of kings and Lord of lords, should be suffering like that. We started praying and realized her suffering was from the oppression of some witches, who wanted to punish her. She did self-deliverance and destroyed the works of the witches over her life. She became pregnant again and was led by the Holy Spirit to keep the news of the pregnancy from the public as well as to avoid contact with the witches. She had the baby safely and became pregnant a second time. She used the same strategy and delivered another healthy baby.

Emotional oppression means a strong feeling of inadequacy; one feels less than capable of handling the daily pressures of life. This may manifest as psychological or behavioral changes. Everything becomes overwhelming, and such a person has nothing good to say. The victim will complain about everything and anything; simple occurrences become exaggerated into looming disasters. Well-meaning statements are interpreted otherwise, and such a person sees nothing good in himself or herself. He or she can't accept compliments with gratitude because he or she doesn't feel worthy of anything good or special.

Mental oppression is something many people can easily relate to; they realize the devil is oppressing them. This oppression relates to experiences of the mind. A person in this state finds it difficult to get rid of a crippling thought or feels powerless in stopping himself or herself from a troublesome or unwholesome action. This may present itself in such manners as inability to stop worrying, even when it's evident there's nothing he or she can do to avert the situation. Another example is fear of different things he or she knows are beneficial, but fear incapacitates him or her from benefiting from them. Unforgiveness can be a mental oppression, when he or she is aware of the need to forgive, but he or she cannot let go. Sadness becomes despair when the devil steps in, and it becomes mental oppression. The devil can turn an ordinary emotion to mental oppression, and the list can go on and on.

Spiritual oppression is the most common oppression by the devil, and it is also the least detected of all forms of oppression. When one is no longer spiritually alert, it's easier for the devil to start oppressing in other areas as well. This can be identified by a lack of desire for the things of God. When praying becomes difficult or reading the word of God no longer interests a Christian, you know you need to pray and do the things of God. You desire to do these things, but it's just impossible to make yourself do them. Possibly, the devil is oppressing you when you find yourself struggling or lack the joy in doing such things, especially if you used to enjoy and love them at one point. There used to be a time when there wasn't enough time in the day to do those spiritual things, like spending time with God, singing praises to God, calling someone to pray with you, and so forth. If you now find yourself struggling, it's time to identify the problem. The goal of the devil is spiritual death, but he also attempts physical death to stop us from doing the work of God.

The example that comes to mind is that of a young man I will refer to as Frank; a family member had a dream that he had died an untimely death, but he was a new father. The dream was narrated to him on a Thursday while he was on his way to a work-related retreat. He was at the airport and afraid of boarding the plane, so he called for prayer. We prayed against this death using the word of God in Isaiah 43:4. "Since you were precious in My sight, You have been honored, And I have loved you; Therefore I will give men for you, And people for your life."

The word of God worked in a way we didn't expect. While at the retreat in the hotel, they were relaxing in the evening. He was playing chess with a colleague by the pool, and another colleague was swimming. The one swimming drowned while they were engrossed with the game. The police had to question all of them, but it was indeed an accidental drowning. We were appalled by the fact that the Bible passage had literally worked in favor of him. An unbelieving guy had died in his place that weekend. We all thought the oppression was over, but we became troubled when he started getting into deadly accidents, but the grace of God saved him several times. The last straw was when armed robbers shot him; a bullet was lodged very close to his jugular vein. The doctors decided to leave the bullet alone because trying to remove it was more dangerous. There was a possibility that the bullet could shift and puncture the vein, and he could bleed to death if they tried to remove it. It dawned on me that we were dealing with the spirit of death; it was following him around, trying to kill him and cut his life and ministry short. Two of us came alongside him, and he did self-deliverance; he has been okay and safe since then. It's our responsibility to make sure we don't suffer spiritual or physical death by the oppression of the devil.

Sickness

Sickness is defined as ill health, which is synonymous with disease, ailment, disability, affliction, weakness, impairment, unhealthiness, unsoundness, mental disorder, madness, neurosis, psychosis, insanity, and many others.

Sickness can have its root in a pathological disorder, but it can also have its root in spiritual affliction. There can also be a progression from one system of the body to the other. I have a good example with an experience I had with sadness, which was secondary to going through a divorce. It persisted and became depression, wherein I was weeping all the time. I had no interest in things I used to love. I cried out to the Lord for help, and I remember the Holy Spirit told me to snap out of it before my problem became clinical depression. It dawned on me that sadness can become deeper and progress to clinical depression, requiring prolonged medication.

These different roots of sickness were exemplified in the Bible when Jesus healed different people by different methods. He knew the source of each sickness and dealt with them accordingly.

Jesus healed a paralyzed man just by asking him to move a hand.

> And He entered the synagogue again, and a man was there who had a withered hand. So they watched Him closely, whether He would heal him on the Sabbath, so that they might accuse Him. And He said to the man who had the withered hand, "Step forward." Then He said to them, "Is it lawful on the Sabbath to do good or to do evil, to save life or to kill?" But they kept silent. And when He had looked around at them with anger, being grieved by the hardness of their hearts, He said to the man, "Stretch out your hand." And he stretched it out, and his hand was restored as whole as the other. (Mark 3:1–5)

Jesus didn't have to do or say anything more than "Stand up and stretch thy hand," and he was healed. The root of that paralysis was likely pathological, such as brachial plexus injury or stroke.

A woman's issue of blood was healed just by touching Jesus's garment.

Now a certain woman had a flow of blood for twelve years, and had suffered many things from many physicians. She had spent all that she had and was no better, but rather grew worse. When she heard about Jesus, she came behind Him in the crowd and touched His garment. For she said, "If only I may touch His clothes, I shall be made well."

Immediately the fountain of her blood was dried up, and she felt in her body that she was healed of the affliction. And Jesus, immediately knowing in Himself that power had gone out of Him, turned around in the crowd and said, "Who touched My clothes?"

But His disciples said to Him, "You see the multitude thronging You, and You say, 'Who touched Me?'"

And He looked around to see her who had done this thing. But the woman, fearing and trembling, knowing what had happened to her, came and fell down before Him and told Him the whole truth. And He said to her, "Daughter, your faith has made you well. Go in peace, and be healed of your affliction." (Mark 5:25–34)

This woman's long-standing bleeding problem was possibly

another pathological disease, such as fibroid in the uterus, and it was healed just by a touch on Jesus's garment. The touch released the power that stopped the bleeding instantaneously, and Jesus acknowledged the released power. Now let us look at the next two examples, which Jesus addressed differently.

A mad man was healed by casting out a spirit from him.

> And when he was come out of the ship, immediately there met him out of the tombs a man with an unclean spirit,
>
> Who had his dwelling among the tombs; and no man could bind him, no, not with chains:
>
> Because that he had been often bound with fetters and chains, and the chains had been plucked asunder by him, and the fetters broken in pieces: neither could any man tame him.
>
> And always, night and day, he was in the mountains, and in the tombs, crying, and cutting himself with stones.
>
> But when he saw Jesus afar off, he ran and worshipped him,
>
> And cried with a loud voice, and said, what have I to do with thee, Jesus, thou Son of the most high God? I adjure thee by God, that thou torment me not.

For he said unto him, Come out of the man, thou unclean spirit.

And he asked him, what is thy name? And he answered, saying, my name is Legion: for we are many.

And he besought him much that he would not send them away out of the country.

Now there was there nigh unto the mountains a great herd of swine feeding.

And all the devils besought him, saying, Send us into the swine, that we may enter into them.

And forthwith Jesus gave them leave. And the unclean spirits went out, and entered into the swine: and the herd ran violently down a steep place into the sea, (they were about two thousand) and were choked in the sea.

And they that fed the swine fled, and told it in the city, and in the country. And they went out to see what it was that was done.

And they come to Jesus, and see him that was possessed with the devil, and had the legion, sitting, and clothed, and in his right mind: and they were afraid. (Mark 5:2–15)

This man could be described as a psychiatric patient who could have been suffering from an uncontrolled psychosis. Jesus addressed it as a spiritual ailment, not a pathological one.

A boy with seizures was healed by casting out a spirit from him.

> Then one of the crowd answered and said, "Teacher, I brought You my son, who has a mute spirit. And wherever it seizes him, it throws him down; he foams at the mouth, gnashes his teeth, and becomes rigid. So I spoke to Your disciples, that they should cast it out, but they could not."

> He answered him and said, "O faithless generation, how long shall I be with you? How long shall I bear with you? Bring him to Me." Then they brought him to Him. And when he saw Him, immediately the spirit convulsed him, and he fell on the ground and wallowed, foaming at the mouth. So He asked his father, "How long has this been happening to him?"

> And he said, "From childhood. And often he has thrown him both into the fire and into the water to destroy him. But if You can do anything, have compassion on us and help us."

> Jesus said to him, "If you can believe, all things are possible to him who believes."

Immediately the father of the child cried out and said with tears, "Lord, I believe; help my unbelief!"

When Jesus saw that the people came running together, He rebuked the unclean spirit, saying to it, "Deaf and dumb spirit, I command you, come out of him and enter him no more!" Then the spirit cried out, convulsed him greatly, and came out of him. And he became as one dead, so that many said, "He is dead." But Jesus took him by the hand and lifted him up, and he arose. (Mark 9:17–27)

This is the same case discussed under affliction. It was a case of seizures, and Jesus treated it as a spiritual problem, not a pathological one. He cast out a spirit instead of just speaking into his life like he did at some other times. I remember that a dear brother was sick for a long time, and the doctors tried different treatment methods, but there was no success. We grew worried that he was going to end up on dialysis or die. I decided to ask for the root of this problem, and I had a dream that the police had arrested this brother and put him in jail. His mom went to the police station, and immediately they saw her. The police started apologizing and said they hadn't known he was her son; they released the bother. I didn't know the meaning clearly, but I knew someone in jail was in bondage and needed to be released. I shared the dream with others, and we prayed a prayer of deliverance for him, casting out every spirit that held him captive. We also sent someone to go and bring the elderly mother to pray for him. The doctor's plan of treatment worked after the prayer; he was discharged and recovered completely.

Obviously, Jesus knew the source of different sicknesses or ailments, and he always knew what to do. We also need to learn from our Lord's example and apply the same principle all the time.

Possession by the Evil Spirit

To have a good understanding of this problem and to differentiate it from other forms of spiritual affliction by the devil, we need to clarify the terms *possess* and *possession*. *Possess* is translated in the English dictionary "to have as property, own, to enter into and control firmly." *Possession* is also translated as "control or occupancy of property, ownership, domination by something." When someone is possessed by a spirit, that spirit has ownership of the person, lives inside that person, and has control. The person may think he or she is the captain of his or her soul, but the truth is, the spirit is the captain of that soul. However, some spirits are just in control of some aspects of the person's life, and the spirit will limit the person's fruitfulness or progress in that area. In most cases, the spirit has a legal ground to be in that person, and the victim is referred to as a legal captive. This could be through actively opening the door for the spirit or the result of an automatic generational ownership. The best example is when Christians dedicate their children to Jesus Christ at birth or at one point or other. Such children belong to Jesus until they reach the age of accountability, when each is expected to make a personal decision to give his or her life to Jesus or veer away from Jesus.

"For the unbelieving husband is sanctified by the wife, and the unbelieving wife is sanctified by the husband: else were your children unclean; but now are they holy" (1 Corinthians 7:14).

The child of a Christian is set apart for the Lord and shielded from the godlessness around him or her by the faith and grace on the life of the believing parent. Now let us apply this to another parent, who happens to be a worshipper of an ungodly spirit as is prevalent in some countries. Some people worship the god of water, the god of thunder, the god of dead ancestors; and some worship the devil himself. These gods or idols are controlled by some spirits. The spirit the person worships has the ownership of him or her, and the child of that person automatically inherits the spirit by virtue of ownership upon his or her life due to association with the spirit. Some grew up, encountered Jesus, gave their lives to Jesus Christ, and became Christians; yet these spirits still claim ownership of their lives. Such evil spirits will continue to hinder the spiritual growth of the Christian, causing unfruitfulness and barrenness in many areas that extend beyond having children. The manifestation of such legal ownership can present a pattern in a family. When you see a family with two or three married couples who are barren or you see two or three adult children who are unmarried in a family, you can be sure there is something wrong with such a family.

Problems can also manifest as a behavior pattern, such as anger running in a family. I have firsthand insight into the legality of ownership of a contrary spirit over a Christian's life when I started dating. I dated a few men, I received three marriage proposals along the line, and I accepted each, but I broke off each relationship for different reasons. The last engagement I broke off was just days before the weeding, and it was a big embarrassment for my family, as I reported in the introduction.

During prayer time, I kept receiving the words *leviathan spirit*. I had no clue what they meant. I couldn't recall hearing them or reading about them, but I was sure my problem stemmed from this spirit. I did my research and found it was a water spirit, and I remembered that my mother told me she was barren during the first few years of her marriage. Before she became pregnant the first time, she was instructed to worship and make sacrifice to one of the water gods. The water god was housed in a mud house, which was falling apart, and she and her friend cleaned the house, restored it, and filled the pot in the house with fresh water. I also remembered that once when I was sick, my mother was advised to sacrifice to the god of water, and she used a hen to make the sacrifice. The Holy Spirit made it clear to me that I was indeed a Christian, but this water spirit had a legal right over my life, because my mother had made a request for children from her, and all the children belonged to that spirit. I accepted Jesus Christ as my savior but didn't deal with the spirit that claimed rightful ownership over my life. Jesus referred to this when he was accused of casting out demons by the power of the devil.

"Or else how can one enter into a strong man's house, and spoil his goods, except he first binds the strong man? And then he will spoil his house" (Matthew 12:29).

A second example is another young lady. I will refer to her as Isabella; she is a short lady but also under the normal weight for her height. She couldn't gain weight and reported that she had been the same body weight for ten years and just looked like a child when she was about twenty-nine years old. She also had difficulty with dating, and relationships weren't leading to expectations. She was instructed to pray for the cause of these problems. Isabella did come back and reported that she had seen one of the pagan gods following her around and calling her by name. We investigated to see whether the parents or generations before her had served and worshipped this pagan god, but they hadn't. We came alongside her, and she did self-deliverance. Within a few days, she noticed that people were complimenting her on her looks—the way she dressed, her hairstyle, and so forth. The aunt who worked with her also attested to the fact that she had blossomed. Every dress she wore was very beautiful on her, and everyone saw her beauty now. Isabella's younger brother said she had never been this beautiful in her life.

She met a man at the bus stop where she had been standing every day to catch a bus for years. The man also used to stand at the same bus stop daily, but they had never met prior to the self-deliverance. They got married after a few months. Six years after the marriage, when she had the third child, the mom came to visit. During conversation she discovered the connection with the pagan god. The mom narrated that she'd had a few miscarriages before getting pregnant with her. In her quest to save the baby when she was pregnant with Isabella, she had gone to the priest of that pagan god; he had done some charms to make the pregnancy reach full term. The story clearly shows the reason this pagan god was still following her, even though she had been in Christ since about five years old, and the parents had also become Christians.

Isabella had been given to the pagan god for protection while in the womb. No one went back to say, "It is over. She now belongs to Jesus." The spirit of this pagan god had been hindering this girl from enjoying the blessings of God for over twenty years, and he had done so legally.

I am going to give another example of a friend and sister in Christ, whom I will call Faith. I have known her for eight years, and she migrated to this country two years before me. When I got to this country, we started discussing the reasons she was still unmarried. I asked her to pray and ask God to reveal the cause of the problem. She called back to report that she remembered an occurrence that had happened before she became a Christian. Her father had been the high priest of a pagan god; he had taken her to another priest to find out which man she should marry, because a few men were trying to date her. This priest said she was going to die if she got married, so he made a charm with a bird and asked her to eat it with an alcoholic drink. She didn't marry any of the men and later became a Christian. We realized the bird she had eaten was responsible for her inability to get married now that she was a Christian.

This was a spiritual problem; there must have been a transference of a spirit through the charm and bird. The spirit had been given authority over her life when the priest was asked to prevent her from death. The spirit prevented death but also stood in the way of her getting married. I came alongside her to do self-deliverance, and good things began to happen. Faith started dating a Christian man from her church; she reported that she had been going to the same church for three years, and the man had been in that church all along but hadn't shown any interest in her up to this point. They got married within the year.

Every Christian, young or old in the faith, male or female, needs to address the issue of sole ownership of his or her life. You don't want any contrary spirit vying for ownership and dominion in your life and hindering the power of Jesus in any way. The examples I narrated above were of a direct legal ownership, but there can be a generational transfer of ownership, as I will expound on with the next example.

A coworker introduced me to a young Christian lady, who felt we shared the same faith, and I could talk to her and encourage her. She was having different problems. She was a Ghanaian but had moved to Europe with the intention of staying and working. Nothing seemed to be working out for her; she had no job because she had no working permit. She had written a book but couldn't find a publisher. She was in her thirties but had no husband or children; she had left her home country and her support group. She had no family in the country and was staying with different friends. Her relationship with her friends also wasn't ending amicably, so she moved from place to place. When I started talking to Theresa, she was broke and wanted to borrow money for rent. She was able to get a cheap place and moved in with a lady who was looking for a roommate; the lady asked her to leave in less than two months. She needed more money to rent an apartment by herself, and I started praying that something would work out for her. She was babysitting but could feed only herself. I also asked God why things were so difficult for her, even though she was a Christian.

I received two answers concerning her problems. The first was that she had a spirit of disobedience. The second was in the form of a dream, which is a revelation. I was taking her somewhere and was the one driving. Suddenly the hood of the van opened and blocked my view, and I couldn't see the road. I was praying frantically while I steered off the road to the shoulder. I turned to her and asked her, "What type of spirit is causing everyone helping you to be a failure?" While I was still asking, I looked up and saw a pagan god of the ancestral spirit and it dressed up as a masquerade as they usually do in that part of her country. He was dressed in his full regalia with his entourage following and they came to the driver's side window. But I woke up before I could talk to the masquerade (spirit).

The following day, I called Theresa and narrated the dream. She was familiar with it and nonchalantly explained to me that the grandmother's family had had a festival of celebration, whereby the masquerade (spirit) came out and paraded the whole village before her mother was conceived. When she was born, they did the same. It was a story narrated to her and her siblings many times, and to them it showed how special the birth of their mother was. The spirit of the masquerade had a rightful claim of ownership over the life of the mother and by extension a transference of ownership to her children and possibly succeeding generations to come. She became a Christian but didn't address the issue of legal ownership of the spirit of this masquerade over her life. She wasn't even aware that the spirit could cause any problem.

The same is applicable to many Christians today. Many are unaware of what they are dealing with. Many Americans today can trace their DNA to multiple nationalities. It's almost impossible to know what all these ancestors did, what gods they worshipped, and what spirits were transferred through different generations. The story of Theresa didn't end well for two reasons: She said something kept telling her to stay away from me; she just didn't see anything wrong with her because she had a good job back in her country. She felt the challenge she faced was only because she was in Europe. I wanted her to do self-deliverance regarding the spirit of disobedience. I was getting frustrated by her unwillingness to cooperate, and I made a statement that came to mind, but I didn't know why. I asked, "Why do you allow the spirit of disobedience to sit on your shoulder?" She responded by saying that a pastor had once told her that he saw a monkey sitting on her right shoulder. There was no physical monkey that could be visible to the naked eyes; it must have been a demon in the form of a monkey. She just didn't believe anything could hinder her if she was in Christ. She couldn't pay her rent and had to go to another friend. I learned from the coworker that she later left Europe to go to another country or continent.

Barrenness

The word *barrenness* has come up under different topics, but it is crucial that we discuss it exclusively. It is translated as sterile, unfruitful, and unproductive of result. It is synonymous with childlessness, impoverishment, scarcity, poverty, emptiness, desolation, ineffectiveness, nakedness, worthlessness, unprofitable, and so forth. The list is unending. We can have a mental picture of a life that isn't going anywhere and a person who is laboring and has nothing to show for it. A biblical example that comes to mind is Jabez in the book of Chronicles.

"Now Jabez was more honorable than his brothers, and his mother called his name Jabez, saying, 'Because I bore him in pain.' And Jabez called on the God of Israel saying, 'Oh, that You would bless me indeed, and enlarge my territory, that Your hand would be with me, and that You would keep me from evil, that I may not cause pain!' So God granted him what he requested" (1 Chronicle 4:9–10).

Jabez became honorable compared to his brethren because of his prayer to God. The prayer made it clear that the brethren weren't considered blessed, their coast must have been small and not worthy of awareness. He came from a family that was poor and inconsequential, and to make his matter worse, he was born with sorrow and pain. Nothing surrounding him was joyful or relevant, such that he knew there was a problem, and he wanted to be different from his brethren. What could have been responsible for the predicament in which this family found itself? This problem wasn't limited to just one or two people in the family, because it wouldn't have been an issue to reckon with. There was no one in the family who was different, whom he could aspire to be like. I presume the root of the problem was neither laziness nor lack of goals, because that wouldn't be compelling enough to plague the whole family. One thing was sure; the members of this family were used to this barrenness and felt comfortable or had developed tolerance to the poverty and lack. I am sure that if we look around, we can identify at least one family that seems to fall into this category; in that family you cannot point out a single member who is doing well and prospering. If there is one who seems different and has the potential to be better, something terrible may happen to him or her, such that he or she still ends up like the rest or dies.

The brethren probably believed it was their lot in life to be poor and insignificant in the society until Jabez came along. He changed the state of barrenness of his life and turned the tide around for himself and his immediate family. Jabez made it clear that the state of barrenness could be changed, and it wasn't the will of God for his children. He answered Jabez's prayer to show us that His plans for us are plans of prosperity, so as children of God, we need deliverance from barrenness whenever we are plagued with it.

I saw barrenness manifested in the life of a young Christian lady I will call Flora. I met her at my work, and she adopted me as her sister. She later told me she had fallen in love with me because she had seen a picture of my nuclear family and desired to have a family like that. She was in her thirties, a single woman living with her younger brother. She was working but wasn't making ends meet and couldn't stand on her own. She started college but couldn't even pass the pre-requisite and had to withdraw. She was dating different men, but none lasted more than a few weeks or months. I became tired of praying about the different men after the eighth guy, and I realized the issue wasn't the guys; something was wrong with this lady, and we needed to find out what. We started praying to God to reveal the secret of her problem.

The revelation was that there was this big tree; the root was outside and not in the ground where it can reach the source of nutrients. The root also looked very ugly and disgusting. It was obvious that this tree couldn't be fruitful. We knew there was a need for deliverance from barrenness and this bad root. She needed a new root that would tap into all the blessings available. I joined her in agreement, and she did self-deliverance.

Flora's story is one of the most convincing evidences I have in support of self-deliverance; her life changed overnight. She got a better job that didn't require schooling. She was trained on the job and could afford to rent her own apartment. I remember helping her move in October. She met her husband on the first day of January; she bought a brand-new car in early February and got married in the same month after just six weeks of meeting the man. The couple bought a house in the month of December just before having a baby in the middle of that same month. In twelve calendar months, Flora received every single blessing she desired and had prayed and fasted for more than ten years. She had a baby at age thirty-three years plus. Everyone in the church started using her as a point of contact to pray for himself or herself. They prayed that the Lord, who had answered Flora's prayer, would answers theirs too. I remember one of her friends praying for a year like Flora's year. They tagged that year "Flora's year."

I want to share an example of barrenness as it relates to a lack of fruitfulness in children. This was applicable to the same lady called Faith in the chapter above. She was married at age thirty-two years and was hoping she would get pregnant immediately, but that wasn't the case. Within two years she was getting anxious and consulted a doctor, who told her she had a severe case of fibroid and required a hysterectomy (removal of the uterus). Faith rejected the recommendation and decided to go for a second opinion. The second doctor's recommendation was the same: surgical removal of the fibroid, but some other tests were done. Different tests, however, showed she had other problems and little to no chance of getting pregnant; adoption was recommended.

She was devastated, and we decided to pray, peradventure there was an underlying spiritual problem. We decided to pray a general self-deliverance prayer just because she didn't know any specific spiritual involvement; but while the prayer was still going on, Faith's father called her and scolded her, saying that whatever she was doing spiritually, she should stop. Faith called to say the prayer must be affecting her father negatively, and he was unhappy. The father refused to speak with her; that underscored her belief that her father must have done something that was responsible or had contributed to the barrenness. The prayer worked because the insurance company referred her to another specialist, who did the surgical removal of fibroid; and she got pregnant three months after the surgery. Faith gave birth to three boys within a four-year period.

Habitual Sin or Addictive Sin

Sin has power over the person who is committing the sin more than most people will give it credit. When we look at the definition of sin as an offence against God or a weakened state of human nature, in which the self is estranged from God, we know that sin cannot be as ordinary as we think or assume. When a person starts committing a sin, he or she may have some sort of control whereby he or she can stop for a while and then go back to it. This ability to go on and off gives a false sense of being in charge, but as time goes on, the ability to stop gets more difficult, or the time interval diminishes. Sin is like a tree that grows roots while the grip or hold over the sinner's life gets stronger. The longer the sin has been in one's life, the more difficult it is to break away; just like the older a tree gets, the more difficult it is to uproot it. The word of God shows this comparison with the love of money as the root of evil. Money isn't sinful, but the love of money is; and it has a root that grows and causes various evil practices. This love is what drives people to commit atrocities in their quest to get more money.

Now imagine someone who loves money has been driven to acquire money and has been spending or enjoying it for some time. It's almost impossible to change his or her mind and say, "I don't want to love money, or I am going to stop acquiring it." This is because every sin develops a root and grows in strength and produces evil fruits, which are different for each sin. A good example is lust, which is the root of many sexual sins; as it grows stronger, it gets worse and begins to produce different fruits such as adultery, fornication, abortion, and the like. No female jumps from just lusting in her heart to committing abortion; there is a progression because of growth, and many will attest to the fact that there are times when they wanted to stop but went right back to it. When a sin goes long enough, it becomes a spiritual stronghold that cannot be uprooted physically. Sin opens the door for evil spirits, and the spirits in turn give power to the sin.

The plan of the devil is to separate us from God, and he gets an opportunity to achieve this purpose when someone fails to repent from committing sin. This becomes an open door for the devil to come into the person's life with the spirit of sin. Many habitual and addictive sins have an underlying spiritual cause whereby a spirit is given power to exercise a hold over the sinner's life until the victim is destroyed. I have two examples to share.

A young Christian lady I will call Melody was having problems with lust, and people were praying for her. One of the ladies who prayed had a dream that Melody had resorted to prostitution, and the dream caused everyone to be more intense in prayer. I remember asking her to pray and ask God for the root of the problem. She came back with the report that when she'd prayed to know the root, she remembered a scene where she was sitting in the lobby of an abortion clinic; and there were also some other young ladies sitting there. She reported that another Christian girl had gone for an abortion, and she had called her to give her a ride because her ride didn't show up. She said God impressed upon her spirit that she'd encountered the spirit of lust in that lobby while she was waiting for her friend because some of those girls in the lobby were into prostitution. We were praying, but instead of things getting better, we were getting the message that they would get worse simply because there was a spiritual influence.

The second example is experiential to me. I don't remember when it started, but I was sure I was enjoying a lustful thought, and it was a feeling that could be compared to feeling high because of the desire for more of it. It got out of hand, and I realized it because I felt I no longer had control, and the thoughts were coming when I didn't want them. Moreover, I was afraid I may commit sin. I cried to God for help and remember weeping while I drove. The Lord reminded me of how I'd opened the door to the devil, and the spirit of lust had come in. My husband at that time committed adultery, and I was hurt and wanted revenge. I thought of committing adultery to hurt him in return, and I opened the door for the devil. When you give the devil an inch, he will drag you for two miles. The thought got out of hand, and I could no longer stop because it had become a spiritual problem, not just a thought. The young lady was instructed in self-deliverance, and I did the same. We both received our victories.

These are just a few reasons all children of God need self-deliverance because there is no way of exhausting the list. There are others who will be pertinent to individuals, and only the Spirit of God can expose the root of different problems.

The Weapons of Self–Deliverance:

1. The Word of God
2. The Name of Jesus
3. The Blood of Jesus
4. Prayer and Fasting
5. The Anointing Oils
6. Christian Prayer Partners

The Word of God

The word of God is indispensable in this discussion, because there is nothing else that can be effectively substituted for the word of God. The book of John makes very clear the importance of the word. "In the beginning was the Word, and the Word was with God, and the Word was God. He was in the beginning with God. All things were made through Him, and without Him nothing was made that was made. In Him was life, and the life was the light of men. And the light shines in the darkness, and the darkness did not comprehend it" (John 1:1–5).

The first verse is plainly saying the "Word" is God himself. Anytime you speak the word concerning a situation, you are speaking God directly into the situation. Verse five of this passage also lets us know that when we speak God into a situation, no matter how evil or how much darkness is involved, we are inviting light into the situation. and the light of God is so powerful that no darkness can stand it. It's easy to imagine a big and completely dark room; when someone enters it with a little lit candle, it will penetrate the darkness and break the power of that darkness. Keep on imagining a situation that is comparable to a room that is so dark, massive, and impossible to penetrate that one is lost and completely doomed. Suddenly a big flood light comes in, and there will be an instant disappearance of the darkness. That is the effect of the word of God on darkness. Verse five didn't just say the light shines, but it so shines that darkness must flee. The Lord gave me insight into the effectiveness of the word of God at a trying time in my life. There was a problem that was persistent in my home. I kept praying for so long that I became frustrated and started praying and asking God what was going on and why I wasn't getting results. On one of the nights, I had a dream that I was in my bedroom, but I could hear some commotion in my house, so I went out of my bedroom and saw three demons sitting at my dining table. I saw them from the back and could tell they were demons by their appearances. I was furious and ordered them to leave my house in the name of Jesus. These demons didn't move or flinch; it was as if they didn't hear me. I panicked at that moment because I wondered, *What if they attack me?* So I made a quick and desperate prayer, asking God what to do; and I heard the Holy Spirit say onto me, "Use the word." Now my predicament was, What word do I use? The first word that came to my mind was the verse above, John 1:1; but I said only the first part, "In the beginning was the Word." Before I could say the rest, those demons fled so fast I couldn't believe they had been there a moment ago. This revelation drove home the significance of knowing the word of God and the consequences of being able to use it when circumstances demand it.

The Lord Jesus taught us by example. When He was confronted by the devil, he didn't confront the devil back by his physical power or ordinary utterance. He brought God into the situation by calling on the word. The devil tempted him three times, and each time he brought God into the situation. The devil cannot stand the presence of God; he had to leave.

> Then Jesus was led up by the Spirit into the wilderness to be tempted by the devil. And when He had fasted forty days and forty nights, afterward He was hungry. Now when the tempter came to Him, he said, "If You are the Son of God, command that these stones become bread." But He answered and said, "It is written, 'Man shall not live by bread alone, but by every word that proceeds from the mouth of God.'" Then the devil took Him up into the holy city, set Him on the pinnacle of the temple, and said to Him, "If You are the Son of God, throw Yourself down. For it is written: 'He shall give His angels charge over you,' and, 'In their hands they shall bear you up, Lest you dash your foot against a stone.'" Jesus said to him, "It is written again, 'You shall not

tempt the Lord your God.'" Again, the devil took Him up on an exceedingly high mountain and showed Him all the kingdoms of the world and their glory. And he said to Him, "All these things I will give You if You will fall down and worship me." Then Jesus said to him, "Away with you, Satan! For it is written, 'You shall worship the Lord your God, and Him only you shall serve.'" Then the devil left Him, and behold, angels came and ministered to Him. (Matthew 4:1–11)

My experience and the example from Jesus made me believe that, though there are multiple weapons, the word of God is the number one weapon needed for self-deliverance. I want to back this up with the word of God by the psalmist. He appreciates and praises the name of God but didn't neglect to put the name in the right perspective compared to the word. "I will worship toward Your holy temple, and praise Your name, For Your lovingkindness and Your truth; For You have magnified Your word above all Your name" (Psalm 138:2).

It cannot be overemphasized that every child of God needs to spend time in the word. If the "Word" is God, as John plainly stated, it can be inferred that spending time reading the word of God is as good as spending time with God. The more time you spend with God, the more of God you will receive, and His power will permeate into you. Know the word and use the word.

The Name of Jesus

Jesus is the most powerful name on earth. It is a name that wrought miracles; the devil hears it and trembles. The unbelieving dares to call it in times of need and even receives grace. The Bible clearly and repeatedly emphasizes the power in the name of Jesus. Jesus emphatically authorized his disciples to use his name, even while he was still with them, and went further to challenge them. I feel like Jesus was saying, "Come on, guys, use my name. Try it and see that it will work for you." Nobody will throw a challenge unless he or she is sure of his or her potential. When a boxer or wrestler has been working out and believes in himself that he can beat an opponent, then he will challenge him by calling for a match. Jesus knows there is no power out there that can withstand his power, so he is telling us to put it to a test.

> Until now you have asked nothing in My name. Ask, and you will receive, that your joy may be full. (John 16:24)

> And whatever you ask in My name, that I will do, that the Father may be glorified in the Son. (John 14:13)

> If you ask anything in My name, I will do it. (John 14:14)

Jesus knows the power in his name, and he gave us the authority to use it; and he sealed that promise with his blood, so it is binding. The disciples made good on the promise and repeatedly found it to be true after the resurrection of Jesus, when he was no longer physically with them.

"Now it happened, as we went to prayer, that a certain slave girl possessed with a spirit of divination met us, who brought her masters much profit by fortune-telling. This girl followed Paul and us, and cried out, saying, 'These men are the servants of the Most High God, who proclaim to us the way of salvation.' And this she did for many days. But Paul, greatly annoyed, turned and said to the spirit, 'I command you in the name of Jesus Christ to come out of her.' And he came out that very hour" (Acts 16:16–18).

Many people think the disciples were more powerful than we are because they were with Jesus, but this is Paul using the name of Jesus. He wasn't physically with Jesus; he had been persecuting the Christians and authorizing the killing of Christians. He was worse as an unbeliever than most of us, yet when he came to the knowledge of Christ and his power, he started using the name, and it worked for him. People around Paul saw the effectiveness of the name of Jesus, and they dared to try the name like Paul, though they had no direct relationship with Jesus. "Then some of the itinerant Jewish exorcists took it upon themselves to call the name of the Lord Jesus over those who had evil spirits, saying, 'We exorcise you by the Jesus whom Paul preaches'" (Acts 19:13).

That incident establishes the efficacy of the name of Jesus, and I believe it will work for us currently as Christians just like it did for Paul. "Nor is there salvation in any other, for there is no other name under heaven given among men by which we must be saved" (Acts 4:12). This statement is equally applicable to deliverance. Brethren, there is no name that is more powerful to do the job than Jesus's name.

The Blood of Jesus

The Lord Jesus shed his blood on the cross for a purpose, and the purposes are numerous. To appreciate the importance of the blood, we must first call to mind what the blood did in the Old Testament when the children of Israel were in bondage in Egypt. In his quest to deliver his people, he had to deal with their oppressors in diverse ways, but the last straw that broke the camel's back was the death of the firstborn of both humans and animals of the land. To save his people from death, he gave them a step-by-step instruction on what to do to escape the plague coming on the land.

> Then Moses called for all the elders of Israel and said to them, "Pick out and take lambs for yourselves according to your families and kill the Passover lamb. And you shall take a bunch of hyssop, dip it in the blood that is in the basin, and strike the lintel and the two doorposts with the blood that is in the basin. And none of you shall go out of the door of his house until morning. For the Lord will pass through to strike the Egyptians; and when He sees the blood on the lintel and on the two doorposts, the Lord will pass over the door and not allow the destroyer to come into your houses to strike you." (Exodus 12:21–23)

The destroyer went through the land, and every house where he saw the blood, he couldn't go in, and no destruction or death occurred in that household. The blood was also used for cleansing from sin and redemption. It brings us forgiveness and redeems us from anything that could be holding us captive or in bondage, including curses and the like. It gives us access to the throne of God; we can go in with confidence and ask for whatever we want. When we want to attend a great or special event, we need a pass, and in most cases, it is bought for a price. The ticket to enter the presence of the King of kings and Lord of lords is the blood of Jesus. We must know that nothing can stop us from approaching God directly as long as we have the right to present the blood of Jesus. So, brethren, come on; bring your pass, wave it high, and go into the presence of God directly, with no waiting, need for an appointment, or hindrance whatsoever.

> For the life of the flesh is in the blood, and I have given it to you upon the altar to make atonement for your souls; for it is the blood that makes atonement for the soul. (Leviticus 17:11)

> And according to the law almost all things are purified with blood, and without shedding of blood there is no remission. (Hebrews 9:22)

> Therefore, brethren, having boldness to enter the Holiest by the blood of Jesus. (Hebrews 10:19)

Prayer and Fasting

Praying and fasting are very common in Bible days, and that is one of the reasons the disciples saw the manifestation of the power of God greatly. The Lord Jesus started his ministry with prayer and fasting. He couldn't have been victorious when the devil came to tempt him if he had been feasting and dining. Jesus was prepared for such times as this; he had been fasting before the devil came to tempt him. He was already in a state of spiritual sensitivity; he could easily know the devil was at work. When our bodies are in control, we tend not to be as astute and undoubted with what we are dealing with, and that trait predisposes us to a failure. There is a possibility of second-guessing selves, arguing, or rationalizing instead of dealing with the devil instantly as Jesus did.

> Then Jesus was led up by the Spirit into the wilderness to be tempted by the devil. And when He had fasted forty days and forty nights, afterward He was hungry. (Matthew 4:1–2)

> Then Jesus said to him, "Away with you, Satan! For it is written, 'You shall worship the Lord your God, and Him only you shall serve.'" Then the devil left Him, and behold, angels came and ministered to Him. (Matthew 4:10–11)

Some of us may argue that this was Jesus, the powerful Savior. Yes, it was Jesus, but he was 100 percent human. He was hungry just like we get when we are fasting. He was tempted repeatedly just like when we get tempted. He didn't get frustrated as the temptation escalated, but he became emboldened and asked Satan to leave. Many of us tend to feel defeated and think we cannot win the battle when Satan keeps bombarding us with temptation after temptation. We hear the phrase "I am fighting my demon." That is the deceit of the devil, making people think everyone has a demon he or she is fighting. We aren't supposed to be fighting the demons. It is high time we start praying and fasting to produce the power and boldness required to ask the demons to leave just like Jesus did.

Praying strengthens our spirits, while fasting weakens the body. I was just thinking that the sins most people commit are milder when the physical body is weak from fasting. You just don't have the strength for some activities. You may be irritable from hunger, which limits your strength to argue or fight as much as you otherwise would have done. Many other desires of the flesh are also subdued, and bad habits are broken. Praying and fasting will produce the power to overcome addictions and any activity that is holding us captive, such as alcohol, cigarette, coffee, sex, and so forth.

A few years ago, I was becoming addicted to shopping. I was shopping at the mall every payday. I knew I was having a problem, but I would rationalize and justify my actions. I felt like I worked so hard and should spend some of the money on myself. My friend and I used to say shopping was therapeutic, and when she called while I was at the mall, I would just say I was in therapy. The Lord got my attention that I needed to deal with the problem.

I had a dream that I was so late at the mall that they locked me up inside. I decided I would leave the mall earlier than I used to. The dream repeated itself, and I started praying but couldn't stop. The last dream was that my purse was stolen at the mall while I was shopping. I decided to fast and pray about it, and it kept coming to my spirit that my purse stood for my finances. I knew this addiction would soon affect my finances. Fasting, especially on the days when I went shopping, helped me to overcome this addiction. I was weak and tired from working and fasting that all I wanted to do was go home, pray, and eat. Praying and fasting empower us and boost our spiritual energy to deal with the flesh and the devil.

The importance of prayer and fasting couldn't have been more evident than in the story of the boy with seizures, which was discussed earlier. The disciples were primarily approached by the boy's father, but they couldn't help him. "And Jesus rebuked the demon, and it came out of him; and the child was cured from that very hour. Then the disciples came to Jesus privately and said, 'Why could we not cast it out?' So Jesus said to them, 'Because of your unbelief; for assuredly, I say to you, if you have faith as a mustard seed, you will say to this mountain, "Move from here to there," and it will move; and nothing will be impossible for you. However, this kind does not go out except by prayer and fasting'" (Matthew 17:18–22).

The apostles approached every important event with prayer and fasting. It is best to live a fasting life, such as never eating till you are full or having a specific day in a week when you fast and pray. Start gradually and teach your body to fast, and whenever you feel the hunger, say a few prayers at such times. The Holy Spirit is our helper, and he will help in this case. Start by calling on the Holy Spirit the night before to help you and give you the grace for the following day. Plan and prepare for the number of hours you want to fast; once you decide, write down the prayer points you will address during your fast. You will be surprised by how easy the Holy Spirit will make the exercise for you. Learn to gradually increase the number of hours. If you have any medical issue that contradicts fasting, please consult your medical adviser and work out a plan that won't harm your health.

The people of God need to get back to the basic source of our spiritual strength like the apostles did; they approached every important decision with praying and fasting in contrast to the present-day church, which plans a potluck breakfast, lunch, or dinner with every event. Today's church needs less dining and feasting to claim back its authority and effectiveness in manifesting the power and glory of Jesus, our Lord. The Lord Jesus made it clear in His teachings that fasting was an important element in the journey of discipleship.

> Moreover, when you fast, do not be like the hypocrites, with a sad countenance. For they disfigure their faces that they may appear to men to be fasting. Assuredly, I say to you, they have their reward. But you, when you fast, anoint your head and wash your face. (Matthew 6:16–17)

> As they ministered to the Lord and fasted, the Holy Spirit said, "Now separate to Me Barnabas

and Saul for the work to which I have called them."
Then, having fasted and prayed, and laid hands
on them, they sent them away. (Acts 13:2–3)

The key phrase in Matthew 6:16–17 is "when you fast." It indicates that you must fast; it is expected of us to fast, so He proceeded to teach us what to do at such times. The key phrase didn't say "if you fast," which gives room for making a choice to fast or not to fast.

Praying and fasting put us in a position of advantage; our spirits are better in tune with the Holy Spirit. We can hear from God easier. We can discern the contrary spirits faster, be sensitive to the plan of action, and be empowered to implement it.

The Anointing Oil

The anointing oil is used in the Bible for various reasons including consecration, cleansing, and healing. Both the New Testament and the Old Testament attest to the use of the oil. The Lord himself ordered Moses to anoint Aaron and his sons as priests unto Him. The pouring of oil was to set them apart for the service of the Lord, and it brought the power and authority of God on them. He was also instructed to anoint some objects and places for them to become special, set apart, and holy unto the Lord. These objects and places are no longer ordinary and cannot be used or entered in a disrespectful manner. The holy objects have the seal of ownership by God, and the presence of God is in the holy places because they have been exclusively separated unto him.

And you shall make from these a holy anointing oil, an ointment compounded according to the art of the perfumer. It shall be a holy anointing oil. With it you shall anoint the tabernacle of meeting and the ark of the Testimony; the table and all its utensils, the lampstand and its utensils, and the altar of incense; the altar of burnt offering with all its utensils, and the laver and its base. You shall consecrate them, that they may be most holy; whatever touches them must be holy. And you shall anoint Aaron and his sons, and consecrate them, that they may minister to Me as priests. (Exodus 30:25–30)

When the Lord chose a man to be made a king in Israel, he also commanded him to be anointed with oil, which made the king a distinguished person with the power and backing of almighty God. King David knew this so well because he was anointed several times, and this anointing connoted a special message to him, such as the other blessings that go hand in hand with the anointing. The gravity of the anointing was comprehended and described in one of his songs. "You prepare a table before me in the presence of my enemies; you anoint my head with oil; my cup runs over. Surely goodness and mercy shall follow me all the days of my life; and I will dwell in the house of the Lord Forever" (Psalm 23:5–6).

David felt chosen by God, set apart, and blessed far above his enemies. His anointing had consecrated him to God, and he experienced the presence and power of God. He had been victorious over his enemies, and he had assurance that the endorsement from God would be with him beyond the present time but forever.

The disciples also used the anointing oil in healing while Jesus was still with them. The apostles continued to use the anointing oil, and James recommended it, which is an indication that it persisted after the resurrection.

> And they cast out many demons, and anointed with oil many who were sick, and healed them. (Mark 6:13)

> Is anyone among you sick? Let him call for the elders of the church, and let them pray over him, anointing him with oil in the name of the Lord. (James 5:14)

I am well versed in the use of the anointing oil and have numerous testimonies of the effectiveness of the anointing oil, and I will share a few in this book. My first encounter is related to the story I shared under the topic "the word of God." The demons fled from my house, but I wasn't done. I went to God with numerous questions, such as why and how they had gotten in my home and that I didn't want a repeat of such. One of the instructions I received was to anoint my home with anointing oil daily. Another incident that comes to mind was a sudden burning pain that engulfed my feet one evening; it was sudden and excruciating, and my first instinct was to start screaming the name of Jesus. I immediately sensed in my spirit that it was an attack, so I asked what to do. Anointing with oil came to my mind, and I didn't just anoint in the spiritual way we do, but instead I poured the oil all over my feet. It was amazing; the pain went away as quickly as it had come.

The last experience I must share is about one of my children, who was giving me a tough time in many areas. I was kept on my toes all the time, constantly praying and asking what to do. One day the Holy Spirit told me to start anointing my children with the anointing oil, and I did so a couple of times. I didn't feel the release in my spirit to stop, but the children were already asking me what was wrong and why and how long, so I asked the Holy Spirit again, and He prompted me to take their picture and continue to anoint them through the picture. I did until one day when I realized I had forgotten the instruction, but then peace had started to reign, which was probably why I forgot.

Christian Prayer Partner

Everyone needs a prayer partner, and it's important to find a Christian friend you can trust. Since you are a Christian, it's expected that you will be praying with someone who is like minded so you aren't unequally yoked in prayer. The most important reason in favor of a prayer partner is that self-deliverance involves spiritual warfare. The first chapter teaches that it's a legal transfer of right or title, and taking back what rightfully belongs to one. We must realize it will involve exercise of power, strength, and authority. Having someone at your side, assisting you to take back what belongs to you, will be beneficial and lessen the burden on you. Having more than one is even better. The Bible underscored this statement for us to make good use of it.

"Two are better than one, because they have a good reward for their labor. For if they fall, one will lift up his companion. But woe to him who is alone when he falls, for he has no one to help him up. Again, if two lie down together, they will keep warm; but how can one be warm alone? Though one may be overpowered by another, two can withstand him. And a threefold cord is not quickly broken" (Ecclesiastes 4:9–12).

The success of this endeavor was clearly seen at the war front with the Amalekites where a powerful spiritual leader like Moses couldn't bring the victory alone, and the effective strategy underscored the importance of having friends and partners who will come alongside of you to fight and win. "And so it was, when Moses held up his hand, that Israel prevailed; and when he let down his hand, Amalek prevailed. But Moses' hands became heavy; so they took a stone and put it under him, and he sat on it. And Aaron and Hur supported his hands, one on one side, and the other on the other side; and his hands were steady until the going down of the sun" (Exodus 17:11–12).

Jesus practiced his word at a time of dire need. He didn't face the battle alone. He had his twelve disciples but also a special few he could trust and call on to come alongside him to give spiritual assistance. He also exemplified this principle to us when he was sending the disciples out, especially when he instructed them to cast out the devil. He knew it wasn't advisable to do such things as a lone person.

And He took with Him Peter and the two sons of Zebedee, and He began to be sorrowful and deeply distressed. Then He said to them, "My soul is exceedingly sorrowful, even to death. Stay here and watch with me." (Matthew 26:37–38)

And He called the twelve to Himself, and began to send them out two by two, and gave them power over unclean spirits. (Mark 6:7)

After these things the Lord appointed seventy others also, and sent them two by two before His face into every city and place where He Himself was about to go. (Luke 10:1)

The examples of disciples working together cannot be exhausted, but a few more can be mentioned, such as Paul and Silas, Peter and James, including Aquila and Priscilla. I won't do justice to this topic if I don't review an example of a leader who operated alone; he was highly victorious, but his success was short lived. That is the prophet Elijah. His zeal for the Lord couldn't be faulted, and he knew his God and did exploits in his name, disgracing and causing the destruction of the evil practices of Baal in Israel by calling fire to consume four hundred of Baal's priests. However, as great as he was, a single evil woman sent him down the path of depression that eventually ended his ministry. This is because he felt and acted alone, and there was no one to encourage him and pull him up and out of his fear and despair. "So he said, 'I have been very zealous for the Lord God of hosts;

for the children of Israel have forsaken your covenant, torn down your altars, and killed your prophets with the sword. I alone am left; and they seek to take my life'" (1 Kings 19:10).

Life Application

Self-deliverance achieves the same purpose, and the method is the same for every condition, but the weapon of choice is different for each condition. Therefore, it's important to be sure of the condition that needs to be addressed at a time. Prayerfully identify and categorize the problem. Is it a sickness, addictive sin, or oppression? You can now choose the applicable method of self-deliverance from the ones listed below.

Curses

This plan of action is applicable for all curses, including generational curses and externally invoked curse.

1. Repent of all sins and bring them under the blood of Jesus.
2. Repent for the sins of your parents and grandparents on all sides up to the fourth generation; bring them under the blood of Jesus.
3. Remove every curse that may be in operation in the name of Jesus.

4. Use the word of God appropriately. Galatians 3:13 is applicable. "Christ has redeemed us from the curse of the law, having become a curse for us for it is written, Cursed is everyone who hangs on a tree."

5. Plead the blood of Jesus on yourself.

Sample Prayer

I repent of my sins, and I ask that you will forgive me. I repent of the sins of my parents and grandparents on both sides, even to the third and fourth generations. I ask that you will forgive and not visit their sins upon me, in Jesus's name. I remove every curse and put an end to its operation in my life, because the word of God says Jesus had redeemed me from the curse of the law. Cursed is everyone who hung on a tree. Jesus did it for me, and I am free in the name of Jesus. I plead the blood of Jesus on me, and I receive the manifestation of every blessing he purchased by his blood in my life, in Jesus's name, amen.

Begin to thank and praise God. You can also repeat the prayer on a daily basis until you begin to experience the assurance and confidence that it has been perfected.

Oppression by the Evil Spirit

It's good to address all the ramifications of evil oppression together, because oppression in one area usually spills over to others. Oppression in one area can also manifest in another.

1. Repent of every sin that may be the cause of this oppression.

2. Remove every curse that may be the underlying problem.

3. Rebuke all the contrary spirits at work in every area of your life.

4. Cast out the evil spirits from your life into eternal captivity.

5. It's good to deal with the agent of the devil here (send back to sender whatever the oppression was supposed to achieve).

6. Use the appropriate word of God. Matthew 17:18; Isaiah 54:17; Psalm 35:7–8; and Isaiah 54:14 are applicable for this exercise.

7. And Jesus rebuked the demon, and it came out of him; and the child was cured from that very hour. (Matthew 17:18)

No weapon formed against you shall prosper, and every tongue which rises against you in judgment you shall condemn. This is the heritage of the servants of the Lord, and their righteousness is from me, says the Lord. (Isaiah 54:17)

For, without cause they have hidden their net for me in a pit, which they have dug without cause for my life. Let destruction come upon him unexpectedly, and let his net that he has hidden catch himself; into that very destruction let him fall. (Psalm 35:7–8)

In righteousness you shall be established; you shall be far from oppression, for you shall not fear; and from terror, for it shall not come near you. (Isaiah 54:14)

8. Receive your healing in all areas (spirit, soul, and body), whether physical, emotional, mental, or spiritual.
9. Anoint yourself with oil.

Sample Prayer

I repent of every sin, and I bring it under the blood of Jesus.

I break the power of every curse that may be in operation in my life in the name of Jesus. I rebuke you, devil, and cast you out of my spirit, soul, and body in the name of Jesus. I put an end to all activities of the devil because the word of God says I will be far from oppression or terror; it shall not come near me. Jesus rebuked the devil in the life of the boy with seizures, and he was delivered and healed instantly. I am delivered and healed of every physical, emotional, spiritual, and mental oppression right now in the name of Jesus. I pray against every agent the devil is using to oppress me and decree that you will fall into your own pit and be caught by your own net; no weapon formed against me shall prosper according to the word of God in Jesus's name.

Start praying this prayer and anointing yourself daily as a sign of separation to the Lord and as a way to establish that you are the property of the Lord; the devil cannot come near you. You can keep doing this until you feel sure in your spirit that it is accomplished.

Sicknesses

We already established that some sicknesses may be the work of the devil or the manifestation of a curse, especially a generational curse or an externally invoked curse. It isn't mandatory that we do a spiritual diagnosis to determine the causative effect of a sickness. We all want to enjoy good health in our bodies, and we won't assume that whatever illness we are suffering from is just a pathological disease. While we may be receiving medical treatment, let us also address the possibility of a spiritual underlying factor.

1. Repent of every sin that may be responsible for this sickness.
2. Remove every curse that may be the underlying problem.
3. Rebuke and cast out all the spirits attacking the body and causing sickness. Send them into eternal captivity.
4. Use the word of God, which is relevant to sickness. These are a few good Bible verses I use all the time: Exodus 23:25; Isaiah 53:5; and James 5:14–15.

So you shall serve the Lord your God, and He will bless your bread and your water. And I will take sickness away from the midst of you. (Exodus 23:25)

But He was wounded for our transgressions he was bruised for our iniquities; the chastisement

> for our peace was upon him and by His stripes we are healed. (Isaiah 53:5)

> Is anyone among you sick? Let him call for the elders of the church, and let them pray over him, anointing him with oil in the name of the Lord. (James 5:14–15)

5. Anoint the body with the anointing oil.

Sample Prayer

I repent of every sin, and I bring it under the blood of Jesus. I break the power of every curse that may be in operation in my body in the name of Jesus. I rebuke you, devil, and cast out every spirit that is causing sickness into eternal captivity in the name of Jesus. I put an end to every sickness in my spirit, soul, and body because the word of God says the Lord will take away disease from me. By the stripes of Jesus I was healed, and the prayer of faith will heal the sick. I am healed in Jesus's name.

Start using the anointing oil to anoint yourself daily until you see results. You may notice that the sickness will go away completely, but it may also become effectively controlled by the medical treatment; and you will start enjoying good health.

Possession by the Evil Spirit

The weapons of self-deliverance for this case differ a little bit; they are secondary to the fact that the spirits in this case have legal authority. The change of ownership must be established before the spirits can be cast out. The Holy Spirit gave me specific terminology to use to address the spirits in this case, and that word is *divorce* and to declare the change of ownership. The moment I gave my life to Jesus Christ, there was a change of ownership and lordship that must be declared and established openly.

1. Divorce every spirit that may be vying for ownership and lordship over your life.
2. Declare Jesus as your God and Lord.
3. Order every spirit to depart immediately and enthrone Jesus.
4. Use the word of God accordingly. These Bible verses are appropriate: Isaiah 49:25 and Romans 10:9.

   "But thus says the Lord: even the captives of the mighty shall be taken away, and the prey of the terrible be delivered; for I will contend with him who contends with you, and I will save your children" (Isaiah 49:25).

   "That if you confess with your mouth the Lord Jesus and believe in your heart that God has raised Him from the dead, you will be saved" (Romans 10:9).

5. Plead the blood of Jesus on yourself.
6. Anoint yourself with anointing oil.

Sample prayer

I come in the power that is in the name of Jesus. I divorce every spirit that isn't of God, which has been holding me captive. I declare Jesus as my Lord and savior. I reject every spirit that isn't of God. I relieve you of all your works in my life and cast you out into captivity in the name of Jesus. I enthrone Jesus over my life from this day because the word of God says the lawful captive will be delivered and they that call upon the name of the Lord will be saved. I am delivered and saved in the name of Jesus. I plead the blood of Jesus on myself, spirit, soul, and body in the name of Jesus, amen.

Anoint yourself and pray this prayer every day until you feel assured in your spirit.

Barrenness

This is a lack of fruitfulness as discussed earlier, and it is contrary to the plan of God for every child of God. This could have multiple causative effects varying from a curse or sicknesses to addictive sin. The secret here is to know the underlying cause and address it accordingly. The word of God clearly makes it known that it isn't our portion and shouldn't be tolerated. You may need to address this in a multilevel way, such as addressing the barrenness at the curse level or sickness level during the prayer.

1. Repent of any sin that could be responsible.
2. Break the curse that could be in effect.

3. Use applicable word of God, such as Deuteronomy 7:14 and John 15:2.

"You shall be blessed above all peoples; there shall not be a male or female barren among you or among your livestock" (Deuteronomy 7:14).

"Every branch in me that does not bear fruit He takes away; and every branch that bears fruit He prunes, that it may bear more fruit" (John 15:2).

Sample prayer: Lord Jesus, I repent of every sin that may be responsible for barrenness in my life. I break the curse over my life that is causing barrenness in Jesus's name. I destroy every root of barrenness because it is against your word in Deuteronomy 7:14, which says I shall not be barren. I remove every barrenness from my life according to your word in John 15:2. In Jesus's name, amen.

Habitual or Addictive Sin

This was described as a sinful habit than cannot be discontinued voluntarily, since the victim keeps going back no matter how much he or she tries to stop. This deliverance requires determination and perseverance. It is a deliverance prayer that must be prayed as many times a day as he or she is tempted. When I was faced with this problem and asked God for help, the Holy

Spirit told me to cast into captivity the spirits behind the thoughts and desire. The thoughts and desires were strong and frequent, and I remember praying this prayer relentlessly several times a day. I felt it was more than a hundred times a day though it could have been less, but it felt like I was constantly battling with these horrible desires. I don't remember when it stopped, but one day it dawned on me that I hadn't prayed that prayer at all that day, and I was so happy and grateful that my deliverance was complete, and I wept in gratitude to God. The desire came occasionally after that, but I knew the solution and didn't give it a chance to sneak back into my life. You need to deal with habitual or addictive sin by following these steps every time you are tempted to commit the sin.

1. Repent of the sin.
2. Cast the spirits behind the thoughts and desires into captivity.
3. Use the applicable word of God. A good one is 2 Timothy 1:7. "For God has not given us a spirit of fear, but of power and of love and of a sound mind." You may just replace the word *fear* with the sin or addiction you are battling.

Sample prayer

Lord, I repent of this (mention the specific) sin, and I cover it with the blood of Jesus. I cast every spirit behind these thoughts and desires into captivity in Jesus's name. I plead the blood of Jesus on my mind because the word of God said in 2 Timothy 1:7 that the Lord hasn't given me the spirit of fear or lust, but he has given me the spirit of power, love, and a sound mind in Jesus's name.

I would like to acknowledge that as much as it is good to be specific, many people may not be able to diagnose the spiritual problem ailing them. Some Christians aren't at the level of knowing how the Holy Spirit speaks to them. It's something we learn and grow in. This shouldn't deter us from doing this self-deliverance. I have a habit of addressing some issues in a generalized manner. I will start by addressing whatever the problem is by saying it's contrary to the word of God. I will use the example of my job. I see clients at the home care level, and we have times some refer to as the season of abundance, and we are very busy. We also have the drought seasons when clients are scarce. There was a time when it occurred to me that it wasn't right for me to be having seasons of drought in any area of my life. I prayed in this manner:

"Drought and scarcity are contrary to the word of God because the word of God says the Lord is my shepherd and that I shall not want. I come against whatsoever is causing this problem in the name of Jesus. If this is an attack of the devil, I rebuke the devil right now and put an end to his activities in my job and finances. If this is a sin, Lord, I repent of it. Please call my attention to it so I will change my ways. If this is just drought, I reject it; your word says you will open the windows of heaven and pour out blessing if I pay my tithe, so Lord, intervene in Jesus's name."

I remember dreaming that my official phone to receive calls when my employers had clients for me fell off my hands and shattered. I tried to grab it, but my supervisor grabbed it first and fixed it. In real life, my phone was okay, and friends and family were calling me regularly. However, calls weren't coming through on the official line from the people who offered me clients, and this was beginning to affect my finances. When I woke up, I thanked God for the revelation. Though I didn't know the meaning of the dream, I started praying that the angels of God would fix my phone in the spirit and that the Lord would minister to my supervisor and use him to bless me. That was exactly what the Lord did, and things turned around for good. The general prayer led to the revelation. It didn't indicate an attack; it didn't show anything I was doing wrong, and it showed a broken, nonfunctional phone in the spiritual realm. A physically damaged phone cannot function, so it also was a spiritually damaged phone. I didn't know what caused the damage to my phone, but the dream gave me insight into what was wrong. I know that if my phone is shattered in the physical realm, it must be fixed, so I just prayed that it would be fixed in the spirit. We may not know everything, but we will know enough to get a solution to our predicament.

A young lady I was mentoring called me while I was driving and told me the family car was giving them problems and costing them money. The husband's job wasn't going well, and he wasn't getting enough hours. They were under financial stress, but the latest problem was that the husband had gone for a walk and gotten a ticket from the police for jaywalking. They couldn't afford this ticket, and it got her worried as well as made her think there was a problem. I joined her in agreement over the issue by praying the generalized prayer like the one above. While we were praying, the word *tithe* dropped into my mind twice, so when we ended the prayer, I asked her whether they are paying a tithe. She confessed that they weren't consistent and had been writing down how much they owed.

The general prayer opened our eyes to the fact that the issue was what they were doing wrong, and it opened the door for the devil to attack their finances. She and her husband repented and started paying their tithes and paying down on the amount they owed. She called me back sometime later to thank me and report that the husband's job had given him an official car and that they didn't have to use their personal car. In addition, the husband started getting more work hours.

I also recall a time in my life when my son was very young, and I was a few weeks pregnant. The son was sick and running a high fever. We were spending the Christmas holiday with my parents. I took him to the nearest clinic, but the treatment was ineffective. I decided to go back home and took him to the teaching hospital where I worked. The doctors knew me and were very supportive. I was able to read my son's diagnosis, and it was "fever of unknown etiology" (fever of unknown origin). That bothered me, and I started praying and asking God why he was allowing me and my son to suffer. Why couldn't they find out what was wrong? I was weak and throwing up from the pregnancy, and I had to sleep on an uncomfortable chair in the hospital. The Holy Spirit answered me and said, "This is a devourer." I quickly asked why a devourer would attack me, but before I finished the prayer, I remembered how my husband got a contract he'd worked on for six months; and we hadn't paid tithe on the money. Instead we used the money to buy a car. We just thought it wasn't part of our regular income from our professional jobs. The devil didn't think so, and he seized the opportunity to attack. I repented, promised to pay the tithe, and rebuked the devourer from our finances. The prayer was around five a.m. while I was doing my quiet time. The nurse came around at about six o'clock in the morning, and the fever was gone. I told the doctor I knew what was wrong and that he should discharge my son so I could go home and take care of the problem. He refused, but by the next time the nurse came (around noon), the boy was playing and couldn't be kept in the crib safely, so he was discharged. I was surprised that the Lord had honored my promise to pay and forgiven me. The problem of over a week was over in a couple of hours once I took care of the spiritual aspect.

Deliverance for Our Children

When we have the knowledge of what we are dealing with and if it involves our children, we have the authority to do deliverance for them. This is applicable to all the topics addressed above, but there are also many others that aren't limited to adults but can be encountered in children and youth, such as the following:

1. Spirit of rebellion
2. Spirit of lawlessness
3. Spirit of suicide
4. Spirit of disobedience
5. Spirit of hopelessness
6. Spirit of addiction

The word of God mandates the parents to train their children and keep them on the straight path because children are moldable and can be easily influenced in one way or the other. When we begin to see some traits that aren't in accordance with the word of God, it is important to address them both physically and spiritually at the earliest possible time before they become a stronghold. "Foolishness is bound up in the heart of a child, the rod of correction will drive it far from him" (Proverbs 22:15).

Children and youth are also very vulnerable, and simple things can become overwhelming and hopeless to them. Many of them will contemplate suicide when things aren't going in their favor. We should not only establish good communication but also pray against it, which will involve delivering them from the spirits involved in such actions. Most of the times these spirits aren't indwelling but are just around; nevertheless they still need to be cast away from our children. Sexual sins start earlier than many parents realize. Children explore their bodies and at times start meddling in activities that can open the door for some spirits of sexual sins. In some cases, they can be afflicted by some spirits simply due to their proximity to people practicing such sins.

> Flee also youthful lusts; but pursue righteousness, faith, love, peace with those who call on the Lord out of a pure heart. (2 Timothy 2:22)

> Flee sexual immorality. Every sin that a man does is outside the body, but he who commits sexual immorality sins against his own body. (1 Corinthians 6:18)

In fact, it is necessary to pray against these spirits regularly and cast them away from your children, because they encounter these spirits, and you cannot afford to wait till the evil practices begin to manifest before you take necessary actions. I recall that a boy started acting like a girl, and at the beginning it was funny, and the other children laughed about it. I was looking and smiling, but suddenly I had this burden in my spirit, and I stared praying and asking God why I was troubled, and it dawned on me that he wasn't just acting silly, as I had thought. I was witnessing the manifestation of the spirit of Sodom. I called the attention of my friend to it, and we started praying and rebuking the spirit as well as declaring that God had made him a boy, and he would act and function as a boy. We decreed that we didn't want that spirit near our children or in our home. We noticed that the boy stopped the behavior not too long after that.

Preventive Measures

We all need to follow the popular statement that says prevention is better than a cure, which the majority of people think is pertinent to physical health. We can all relate to the effectiveness of prevention of catastrophe compared to finding ways to ameliorate it. Many of us believe in the effectiveness of immunization, and we have seen it cause eradication of some debilitating and fatal diseases in developed countries. I have always applied this principle of prevention to areas of spiritual health, in that I take time to do deliverance prayer over myself and my family, even when I'm not in crisis. Once or twice a year, I pray a general prayer of deliverance for my children and me. I also call it a "cleansing prayer." This is because we can be afflicted in the process of our day-to-day activities. The second reason is brought about by my understanding that when the devil leaves us alone for a season, he always comes back to try again and again. We cannot just live and function on a one-time deliverance throughout our lives. Jesus himself experienced and taught the same lesson.

> And Jesus answered and said to him, It has been said, You shall not tempt the Lord your God. Now when the devil had ended every temptation, he departed from Him until an opportune time. (Luke 4:12–13)

> When an unclean spirit goes out of a man, it goes through dry places, seeking rest, and finds none. Then he says, "I will return to my house from which I came." And when he comes, he finds it empty, swept, and put in order. Then he goes and takes with him seven other spirits more wicked than himself, and they enter and dwell there; and the last state of that man is worse than the first. So shall it also be with this wicked generation. (Matthew 12:43–45).

This last passage is scary to me and keeps me vigilant in making sure the devil has no opportunity to come back into my life and reinforce himself with other spirits and make my state worse. If the devil left Jesus only for a season and looked for an opportune time to return, what do you think the devil is doing to us? He is looking for an opportunity to come back and attack us or our families. "Be sober, be vigilant; because your adversary the devil walks about like a roaring lion, seeking whom he may devour" (1 Peter 5:8).

We cannot be oblivious to the possibility of relapse in our spiritual sanctity. I always compare this to taking a booster dose of a vaccine after some time when the effect of the immunization is wearing off, and the last vaccine is deemed no longer effective to prevent the disease. We need to be wise and take spiritual preventive measures regularly just like we do regarding our physical health.

The Place of Deliverance in the Ministry

I believe God created everyone for a purpose, and in most cases, it is the area of our ministry in the body of Christ. It is our calling in life, and we experience joy and fulfilment when we know the areas and actively participate in them. The success of the ministry depends on our effectiveness and the joy we derive from serving. A prayer warrior or an intercessor feels satisfied and happy when he or she experiences answers to prayers. An evangelist is happy and fulfilled when souls are saved. A very important area of hindrance by the devil is our individual ministry. The devil blocks people from knowing their callings, or he makes them despise their ministry and covet someone else's ministry. The devil doesn't want us to be fruitful or fulfilled in the ministry; that is why many people start strong but gradually stop or quit outright. Many of us can look back at times when we were excited about Jesus, and we told everyone around us about him. We can remember when we prayed about anything and everything. The experiences are different and numerous, but the stories are the same; our participation has diminished, and performance is no longer strong. We all need to do a self-examination of the impediment to our ministry and deal with it accordingly.

In my self-examination, I sometimes couldn't recall sharing about Jesus's love to a single person in three months or more. I also remember times when I knew and felt like I had refrained from praying or reading the Bible. I found it effective to deal with the fear that prevents me from telling people about the love of Jesus. I also clearly remember a time in my life when I was really struggling to pray, and I started asking God for the cause, because praying is my ministry. Not only do I enjoy praying, but I find my fulfillment in praying for people, government, and even nations.

I had a dream that many cats were in my home, coming in and out of the rooms; but in real life I have no pet in my home. I was sure in the dream that my home had been invaded by the spirit of witchcraft. When I woke up, I prayed and asked how the spirit had gotten into my home, and immediately a new TV show I had been watching came to my mind. I went on vacation to Europe to visit my friend; she was watching this Korean television show. I enjoyed it so much that I continued to watch it when I got back home. I became so engrossed in the show that I felt it was addictive. To stop the addiction, I started withdrawing from watching it every day. The dream opened my eyes to the fact that it wasn't just addictive; it had spiritual significance that predisposed me to an attack from the spirit of witchcraft. The consequences were an inability to pray and the difficulty of fellowshipping with

God. That simple television series could have been my spiritual demise.

I had to stop watching the show, which was more difficult for me than I anticipated, since it confirmed to me that the television series wasn't just addictive but had the power to hold me captive. I also needed to rebuke the spirit of witchcraft and any other spirit that was hindering my spirit and ministry. In addition, I had to cleanse my home from the invasion and declared my home as the property of God by anointing my home. I want to recommend that every child of God who had been fervent in the spirit and ministry at one point but is no longer functioning at a meritorious level needs to ask God for what is responsible. If you know, take charge and rebuke and cast out any spirit at work. Even if you don't know, you can still address the unidentified spirits, and you will be victorious.

1. Repent of any sin that could be responsible for an open door.
2. Rebuke and cast out the responsible spirits.
3. Cleanse and cover your mind and home with the blood of Jesus.
4. Use the word of God. Some appropriate verses are Isaiah 54:17 and Psalm 105:14–15.

> No weapon formed against you shall prosper. And every tongue which rises against you in judgment thou shall condemn. This is the heritage of the servants of the Lord, and their righteousness is from me, saith the Lord. (Isaiah 54:17)

He permitted no one to do them wrong; Yes, He
rebuked kings for their sakes, saying, do not touch
my anointed ones, and do my prophets no harm.
(Psalm 105:14–15)

Sample prayer: Lord Jesus, I repent of any action that has
led to my spiritual ineffectiveness in all areas. Forgive me and
cleanse me by your blood in Jesus's name. I rebuke every spirit
that is hindering my relationship with you. I rebuke every spirit
that is impeding my spiritual growth or sabotaging my ministry
in Jesus's name. The word of God says no weapon of the enemy
fashioned against me shall prosper and not to touch his anointed
and or do his prophet harm. I cover my mind, home, and ministry
with the blood of Jesus. I begin to prosper in my relationship with
Jesus and in my ministry from this day forward in Jesus's name.

What Is Your Problem?

You have been reading this book, and up to this point, maybe
your answer is, "I don't know." You cannot identify your specific
problem or how to deal with it. This is common and frustrating,
and it can be a hinderance to achieving the freedom you crave.
I always recommend praying to know the secrets behind the
problem before trying self-deliverance. I'm very specific in my
request and will remind God to reveal the secret to me in a dream;
this is because it is the simplest, most dramatic, and easiest-to-
understand way of knowing spiritual secrets. I also ask God to
make it clear and explanatory like the dreams Joseph and the
shepherds had.

But while he thought about these things, behold, an angel of the Lord appeared to him in a dream, saying, "Joseph, son of David, do not be afraid to take to you Mary your wife, for that which is conceived in her is of the Holy Spirit." (Matthew 1:20)

Then, being divinely warned in a dream that they should not return to Herod, they departed for their own country another way. (Matthew 2:12)

Now when they had departed, behold, an angel of the Lord appeared to Joseph in a dream, saying, "Arise, take the young Child and His mother, flee to Egypt, and stay there until I bring you word; for Herod will seek the young Child to destroy Him." (Matthew 2:13)

Now when Herod was dead, behold, an angel of the Lord appeared in a dream to Joseph in Egypt. (Matthew 2:19)

We can all see that dreams in these cases were not only simple but also commonly used of God. I strongly believe that when we ask, the Lord will make it easy and clear to us in a dream whatever is plaguing us in the spirit, as he did over and over in the biblical examples. We can all recall that God used dreams to talk to many pagan kings in the Bible, such as Pharaoh and Nebuchadnezzar; if he could do that for pagans, he will do so much more for us. We need only to be specific in our request. When the dreams come, we can easily address the issues revealed.

My personal example of many cats in my home was clear enough, even if I don't know what the cats stood for. I knew it wasn't right for them to invade my home, and this bothered me in the dream. I woke up praying that whatever they stood for, I didn't want them in my home and in my life. It was adequate for me to cast them out of my home. However, I could sense in the dream that they stood for the spirit of witchcraft, so I was able to address them categorically. It's okay to address whatever spirit may be represented, even if you don't have a definite understanding of the spirits; those spirits will still be covered under the category of "whatever spirits," and they have no choice but to leave because the Lord will honor that request.

This principle of generalized self-deliverance—that is, addressing whatever spirit is involved in the problem—was used with one of the ladies I befriended at work. She is a very devoted Christian sister, who converted to Christianity from another religion. She wants to be referred to as "Treasure" in this book. I like to talk to her a lot because this gives me an opportunity to help her stand and not go back to her old friends, who are practicing the other religion. During a discussion, Treasure confided to me that every time she had been pregnant, a man she didn't know in real life would come and have sex with her in her dream. She believed he was responsible for her giving birth to female children. She has had five girls but no male child. Treasure and her husband are from Asia, and male children are very important.

I was surprised that she had never shared this story with any of her Christian friends. She was ashamed of such dreams and kept them to herself. I was very sure it wasn't normal for someone who wasn't her husband to be having intimate relationship with her in her dreams. We didn't know what we were dealing with, but we decided to address any spirit that was in action or might have been passed through such dreams. We kept praying, and Treasure became pregnant within six months and had her sixth child, the first son. She didn't plan to get pregnant because she thought she was in menopause. She had the son at age fifty and a few months, and the last girl was already ten years old. You can do self-deliverance, even when you're unsure of spiritual involvement or even the type of spirit you are dealing with. You need to play it safe; assume there is a spiritual connection, and therefore take care of it accordingly.

The Need for Importunity

We are living in an age of swift gratification; every desire is required instantaneously. It isn't our fault; technology has been developing at a rapid pace for ages, and we can no longer remember when we must wait for anything again. Humans have been taught to choose speed over character. This generation will drive instead of walk, we will fly instead of drive, and we will use a microwave oven instead of a conventional oven. This attitude is infiltrating our spirits, and we have inconspicuously become impatient. We find it difficult to persevere in prayer or wrestle in the spirit. We are looking for three steps and seven steps to our breakthroughs. I have suggested that you pray some of the prayers on a daily basis until confidence and assurance of are impressed in your spirit.

There are three main reasons for this suggestion. The first is that everyone who found deliverance persisted. The father of the boy with seizures approached the apostles first, and when he didn't get the answer, he went to Jesus and received his miracle. Jesus said some spirits won't go out except by prayer and fasting. If you are praying and the answer seems delayed, you need to fast as suggested in the previous chapter. Don't stop asking and praying until you begin to see a breakthrough. The second reason is that experience has shown me that in most cases, we are dealing with more than one issue at a time. The Lord will reveal one problem at a time; when you address the first one, you need to pray for revelation of any other one that may be pertinent. When you deal with the issue of spiritual procession, you may then need to deal with a generational curse. You continue until complete deliverance is accomplished, and that is when you begin to live triumphantly. The third reason is that some spiritual problems don't manifest until the appropriate time in the life of the person. The spirit of barrenness won't manifest in a person's life until he or she is at the age of fruitfulness. The spirit of barrenness that prevents having children won't become active until the person is ready to have children. The proposal is that you need self-deliverance at every point in life when you have difficulty and suspect spiritual involvement.

Now What?

Now that you have addressed every area you have need for self-deliverance, it is time to step out and begin to follow the step-by-step instructions and leading of God. There is no longer a hinderance to your victory and prosperity, but the Lord will lead you to lay your hands on something he will use to prosper you.

"The Lord will command the blessing on you in your storehouses and in all to which you set your hand, and He will bless you in the land which the Lord your God is giving you" (Deuteronomy 28:8).

What is God leading you to do? Is it to go back to school, change your eating habit, break away from some relationships, go back to church, start praising him, start serving him in church or community, and so forth? You need to obey because whatever he is asking you to do now will be used to take you to that realm of fulfillment and cause you to live victoriously. "Has the Lord as great delight in burnt offerings and sacrifices, as in obeying the voice of the Lord? behold, to obey is better than sacrifice, and to heed than the fat of rams" (1 Samuel 15:22).

When you do all that is suggested and begin to do what the Lord is asking you to do, there will be a rapid, instant, or gradual transformation in your situation, and you will become living evidence of the greatness and faithfulness of Jesus Christ. I'm sure the evidence in your life will advertise the Lord your God to the people around you.

Conclusion

The Lord surprised me many years ago by showing me the effectiveness of self-deliverance. When I was praying and fasting regarding the last broken engagement, as I explained in the introduction of this book, the friend who had invited me to the prayer retreat received her answer. Immediately we came back, and I didn't hear anything. I went to God on my own, asking for the secret of my problem, and that was when the words *leviathan spirit* kept coming to my mind. I asked God how I should deal with this spirit because I was angry and didn't want it in my life. The Holy Spirit told me to divorce it. I kept praying, "I divorce you, leviathan spirit. I cast you out of my life every day." I prayed this every time I remembered, several times a day. I was passionate about getting rid of it and getting all my blessings back.

This happened toward the end of July. In August, a friend from work informed me that a friend of her husband was asking about me. She felt he was interested in me and that I should start praying. I greeted him in church when he visited our church. I started dating him in August, and he proposed to me in October. While we were planning the wedding, I had a dream that I was pregnant, but at five months, there was a miscarriage. The doctor was upset with me and said this was a precious baby and that this was my third time. I woke up troubled because I was a virgin and couldn't have miscarried three babies. While I was praying over the issue, the Holy Spirit explained to me that engagement is like being pregnant, and getting married is like delivering a healthy baby. I got the understanding that miscarriage at five months meant this engagement would be broken again at five months. I also realized I had missed the opportunity to marry two good men in the past; this was my third opportunity. I didn't want to miss it again.

Prayerfully, we decided to get married before the engagement reached five months. I was married in December of the same year. My family didn't face the shame of calling the wedding off. Many family and friends thought the date had just been moved forward; the majority didn't know the groom was different. I delivered a baby boy nine months later. I was married and pregnant, and I became a mother within fourteen months of doing the first self-deliverance. I became a believer in self-deliverance and have been sharing it with as many as have situations that aren't responding to conventional praying and fasting. Lately I have been making it my first step of action when dealing with many situations. I challenge you as a believer to do this for yourself and your children; you have nothing to lose, even if it doesn't work for you. I can assure you that it works if there is spiritual involvement; you will gain a lot and become a praise to our Lord and a blessing to the body of Christ

Are You a Christian?

Many people believe they are Christians but cannot pinpoint a date when they gave their lives to Christ. The majority of such people were born into Christianity, which means one or two parents are Christians, and they raised their children in the Christian faith. The Bible doesn't support the doctrine of inheritance of faith in Jesus. Jesus preached the gospel of an individual relationship with God. God called us sons and daughters; there is no indication of grandsons and granddaughters in the Bible. The fact that your father is a medical doctor may give you access to a lot of knowledge of the medical practice and some interactions with people in the medical field, but it doesn't make you a medical doctor. It is necessary to say that everyone needs to be responsible for his or her faith in Jesus Christ and have a personal history of when his or her vote was cast for Jesus amid all the gods vying for his or her soul.

> For God so loved the world that He gave His only begotten Son, that whoever believes in Him should not perish but have everlasting life. (John 3:16)

> Behold, I stand at the door and knock. If anyone hears my voice and opens the door, I will come in to him and dine with him, and he with me. (Revelation 3:20)

> That if you confess with your mouth the Lord Jesus and believe in your heart that God has raised

> Him from the dead, you will be saved. For with
> the heart one believes unto righteousness, and
> with the mouth confession is made unto salvation.
> (Romans 10:9–10)

It is paramount to cast your vote for Jesus Christ by acknowledging your sins and confessing them. Ask Jesus for forgiveness, invite him into your life, and declare him as your Lord and savior. I always advise that this date should be saved for reference purposes. The devil is going to challenge your authority at one point in your journey with Christ, and you will remind him of this day in your history when you became a Christ follower and received all the benefits and authority that were obtained for all his brethren and coinheritors.

Sample prayer: Jesus, I acknowledge I am a sinner, and I know you died for my sins. Forgive me for all my sins including the sins I inherited from my forefathers. I invite you into my life as my Lord and Savior from this day forward. I receive all the blessings you purchased for me by your death on the cross. Thank you, Jesus.

This prayer seems very simple, and to some people it may seem inadequate for such a consequential salvation. However, that prayer, when genuinely made, is all the requirement needed to be saved. It is appropriate to say congratulations to whoever prayed this prayer, and if you prayed to assert your salvation; you continue in your journey by following Jesus. If this is your first time of praying this prayer, you are a brand-new Christian; and you will need to find a Bible-teaching church near you to grow in faith and in a relationship with Jesus Christ.

Personal Testimonies

"I can testify to the fact that self-deliverance works. I will give you two important instances in the milestone of my life. The yoke of late marriage and barrenness was destroyed through self-deliverance. In fact, my junior sister had completed childbearing before I got married. One may think that the children will start coming immediately. Doctors told me I should forget about having children. I was advised to adopt, but through self-deliverance prayer, this also became history." —A. O., New York

"I remember what you told me when I was having the fear of accidents. I will pray that I won't have accident, yet the fear and thought won't leave. You taught me that I should cast the fear out in the name of Jesus and send it into captivity. It worked, and I have been using this principle since then, and it keeps working." —P. O., Lagos, Nigeria

"I had a dream while my oldest daughter was a junior in college that a couple of people made her kneel in the middle. They surrounded her and placed hands on her head. I woke up and started praying and fasting, and asked God for the interpretation of the dream. After the fasting and praying, the people involved were revealed. In my mind, I thought that all was well since I had fasted and prayed. The devil is very deceiving. I went about my business until one day my daughter called and said, "Come and get me" and dropped the phone. I could not reach her, and we were worried. We reached the college police department, and the father had to cancel all his appointments and fly to the college to pick her up. She was having various problems and couldn't go back to college. It took a couple of years of joint prayers from family, Christian brethren, and finally deliverance for her to be liberated. The situation has strengthened my faith in the Lord, knowing that with God, all things are possible. The plan of the enemy was for my daughter not to graduate from college, but to the glory of God she graduated. My belief is that if we serve God faithfully, he will show up in all situations and fight any battle on our behalf. God is able, and his mercies endure forever." —B. S., Indiana

Printed in the United States
By Bookmasters